THE NEW GROLIER CHILDREN'S ENCYCLOPEDIA

3

Constellation – Explorer

GROLIER
EDUCATIONAL

Published 1999 by Grolier Educational, Danbury, CT 06816
This edition published exclusively for the school and library market

Planned and produced by Kingfisher Publications Plc,
New Penderel House, 283-288 High Holborn, London WC1V 7HZ

Set ISBN 0-7172-9373-4
Volume 3 ISBN 0-7172-9376-9

The new Grolier children's encyclopedia.
p. cm.
Rev. ed. of: The Grolier children's encyclopedia, 1994.
Summary: A ten-volume encyclopedia presenting illustrated articles, alphabetically arranged, on a wide variety of topics.
ISBN 0-7172-9373-4 (set : alk. paper). -- ISBN 0-7172-9374-2 (v. 1: alk. paper). -- ISBN 0-7172-9375-0 (v. 2: alk. paper). -- ISBN 0-7172-9376-9 (v. 3 : alk. paper)
1. Children's encyclopedias and dictionaries. [1. Encyclopedias and dictionaries.] I. Grolier Educational (Firm) II. Grolier children's encyclopedia.
AG5.N34 1998
031--dc21 98-7378
CIP AC

Printed in France

INTRODUCTION

The word *encyclopedia* comes from the Greek for "all-round education," and *The Kingfisher Children's Encyclopedia* provides just that, in a way that is both accessible and stimulating.

This all-new encyclopedia covers everything from ancient history to up-to-the-minute developments in technology; from animal and plant life on Earth to plans for the next millennium in outer space. Geography, natural history, religion, the human body—all the topics that children explore at home and at school are included here.

We have rejected the "sound-bite" approach to children's reference in favor of more in-depth coverage, which makes this encyclopedia perfect for project work and homework assignments. At the same time, the text is broken up into manageable paragraphs, suitable for both confident readers and younger browsers. Colorful photographs and superb illustrations and maps not only enhance the text, but also encourage readers to find out more for themselves.

Easy access is the key to this encyclopedia. Major subject areas such as ELECTRICITY have been arranged alphabetically, but the encyclopedia also has a comprehensive index so readers can refer quickly to related topics, such as CIRCUITS and SWITCHES.

The encyclopedia has been written and checked by a team of specialist authors and consultants, and produced by a team of editors and designers with years of experience in children's reference. We are confident that it is a work in which children, and parents, can put their trust.

The Editors

Editorial Director
Jennifer Justice

U.S. Consultant
Bill Shapiro

U.S. Editor
Aimee Johnson

Managing Editor
Sarah Allen

Editorial team
Trevor Anderson, Max Benato, Jane Birch, Harry Boteler, Anne Davies, Rebecca Fry, Tracey Kelly, Sarah Kovandzich, Elizabeth Longley, Miren Lopategui, Rupert Matthews, Jayne Miller, Susan Scharpf, Brian Williams

Creative Director
Val Pidgeon

Art Director
Mike Davis

Art Editor
David Noon

Design team
Liz Black, Pete Byrne, John Jamieson, Ruth Levy, Emma Skidmore, Nina Tara

DTP Operator
Primrose Burton

Picture Research
Vencta Bullen, Davina Bullen, Sophie Mortimer, Yannick Yago

Maps
Hardlines

Contributors & Consultants
Sue Aldridge, Sarah Angliss, Max Benato, Martyn Bramwell, Enid Broderick, Tim Brown, David Burnie, Catherine Halcrow, Jack Challoner, Michael Chinery, Maria Constantino, Chris Cooper, Sophie Cooper, Alan Cowsill, Jeff Daniel, David Darling, Dougal Dixon, John Farndon, Sue Gordon, John Graham, Ian Graham, Catherine Headlam, Lesley Hill, Caroline Juler, Anne Kay, Robin Kerrod, J.C. Levy, Keith Lye, Tim Madge, David Marshall, Bob McCabe, Iain Nicolson, Steve Parker, Jane Parker, John Paton, Malcolm Porter, Sue Reid, Meg Sanders, Philip Steele, Richard Tames, John Tipler, Ian Westwell, Brian Williams

CONSTELLATION

Constellations are groups of stars that form recognizable patterns in the night sky. Astronomers have named a total of 88 constellations.

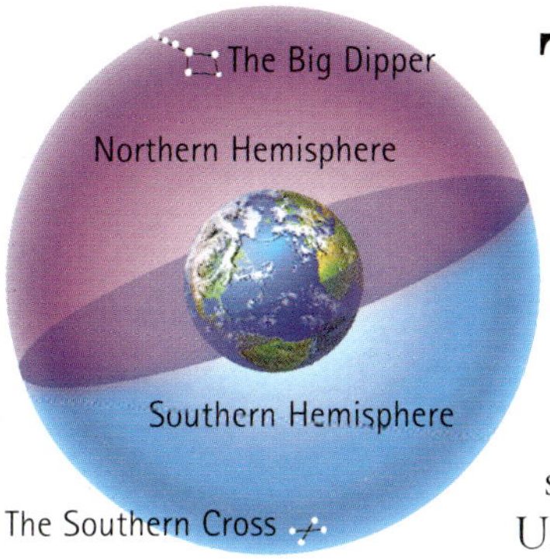

▲ The Northern and Southern Hemispheres are domes of sky seen above and below the equator.

Thousands of years ago, people in Asia, Europe, and the Middle East realized that the stars formed patterns in the sky, and named them after characters and creatures in their lives and legends. By A.D. 300, the Greek astronomer Ptolemy had named 48 constellations. Many of the names he gave them are still in use, including Taurus (the Bull), Ursa Major (the Great Bear), and Andromeda (a mythical Greek heroine). Today, astronomers use the position of the constellations to map the stars.

THE ZODIAC

If we could see the stars during the day, the Sun would pass in front of 13 constellations over the course of the year. The ancient astronomers counted only 12 constellations and called them the signs of the zodiac—claiming that babies born under each sign would have certain traits.

NEAR AND FAR

Stars in a constellation seem close to each other, but are usually far apart. Orion contains the stars Betelgeuse (300 light years from Earth), Rigel (900 light years away), and Mintaka (2,300 light years away). One light year equals 5.88 trillion miles (9.46 trillion kilometers).

MAPS OF THE STARS

Two maps of the constellations are needed because people who live north of the equator (in the Northern Hemisphere) see different stars from those who live south of the equator (in the Southern Hemisphere). The constellations in the center of each map can usually be seen all year round, while those near the edge can be seen only during particular seasons or at certain times of the night.

SOUTHERN HEMISPHERE

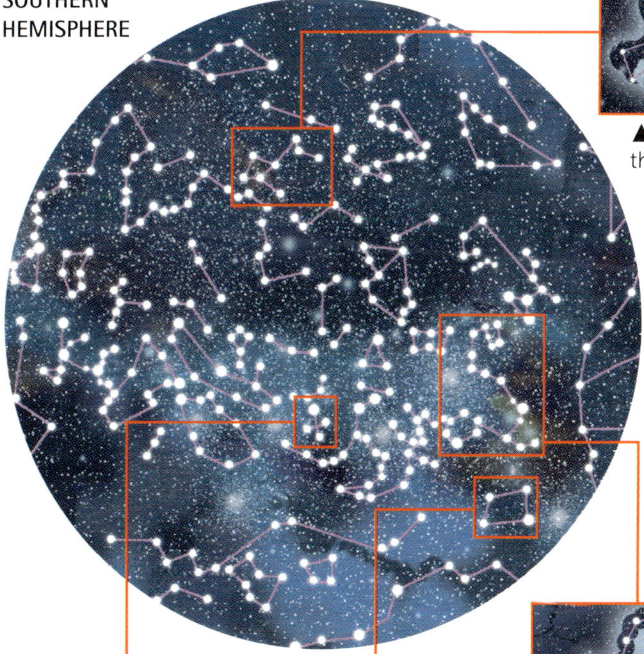

▲ Phoenix, the Fire Bird

▲ Crux, the Southern Cross

▲ Libra, the Scales

▲ Scorpio, the Scorpion

NORTHERN HEMISPHERE

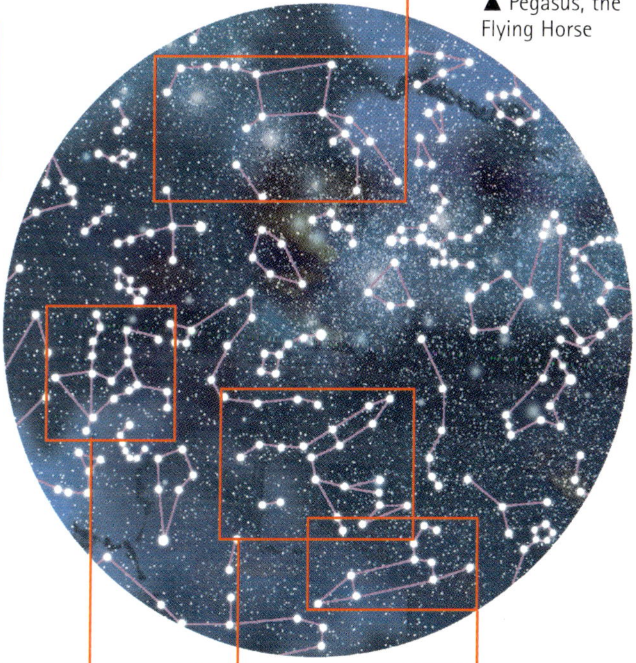

▲ Pegasus, the Flying Horse

▲ Hercules, the Giant

▲ Ursa Major, the Great Bear

▲ Leo, the Lion

SEE ALSO

Astronomy, Galaxy, Myth and legend, Solar system, Star

CONSTRUCTION

Construction is the process of putting something together. This can include houses, skyscrapers, bridges, dams, roads, and even ships.

Bricks are still the most popular construction material in house building.

Carpentry is used to make the main frame, doors, and windows in many houses.

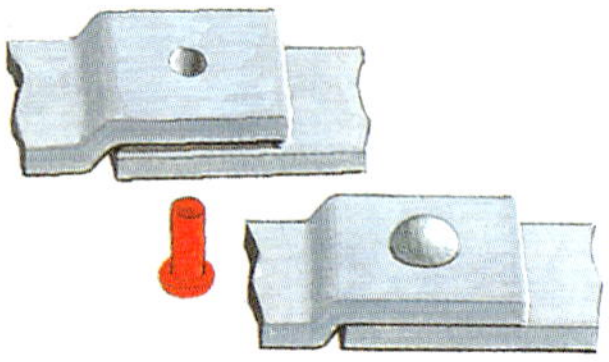

The frames of tall buildings and ships used to be fixed with hot nails, or rivets.

The construction industry is big business—it accounts for 15 percent of all jobs in the United States. The world's largest construction project, building a city in Saudi Arabia in the 1970s, employed nearly 52,000 people.

TRADITIONAL TECHNIQUES

In the past, most construction was domestic. Each family built a house, pens for animals, and dams to irrigate their crops. The materials were usually natural and found locally and included wood, clay, stone, bone, skin, or grass. Work was done by hand.

THE DAWN OF CIVILIZATION

As more complex civilizations developed, so did building skills. The first bricks were made in Palestine in 6000 B.C., and the construction of the pyramids in Egypt required thousands of workers, as well as skilled mathematicians. Ancient cranes were used on Roman building sites.

▲ Hong Kong Harbor Bridge under construction in 1996. The last road section is being lifted from a barge below.

MODERN CONSTRUCTION

The size and height of constructions used to be limited by the skill of the stonemason or carpenter. But from the late 1800s, new techniques using steel frames and molded concrete allowed skyscrapers to be built.

A BUILDING GOES UP

There are two main stages in constructing a building. First, the foundations must be laid below ground to support the structure. Tough materials, concrete (poured in trenches) or steel columns (driven into the ground), are used. The second stage is the construction of the building above ground. Either the walls or a steel frame are constructed first to support floors and other features. Finally, the roof is added.

STEEL-FRAMED CONSTRUCTION

Modern high-rise buildings usually have a steel frame onto which floors and wall panels are bolted. The frame supports the weight of the building so walls can be thin with large windows.

▲ H-shaped, reinforced steel girders are bolted together to form the building's frame.

▲ Metal floor panels are bolted to the frame, then a wire mesh is laid and concrete is poured over it.

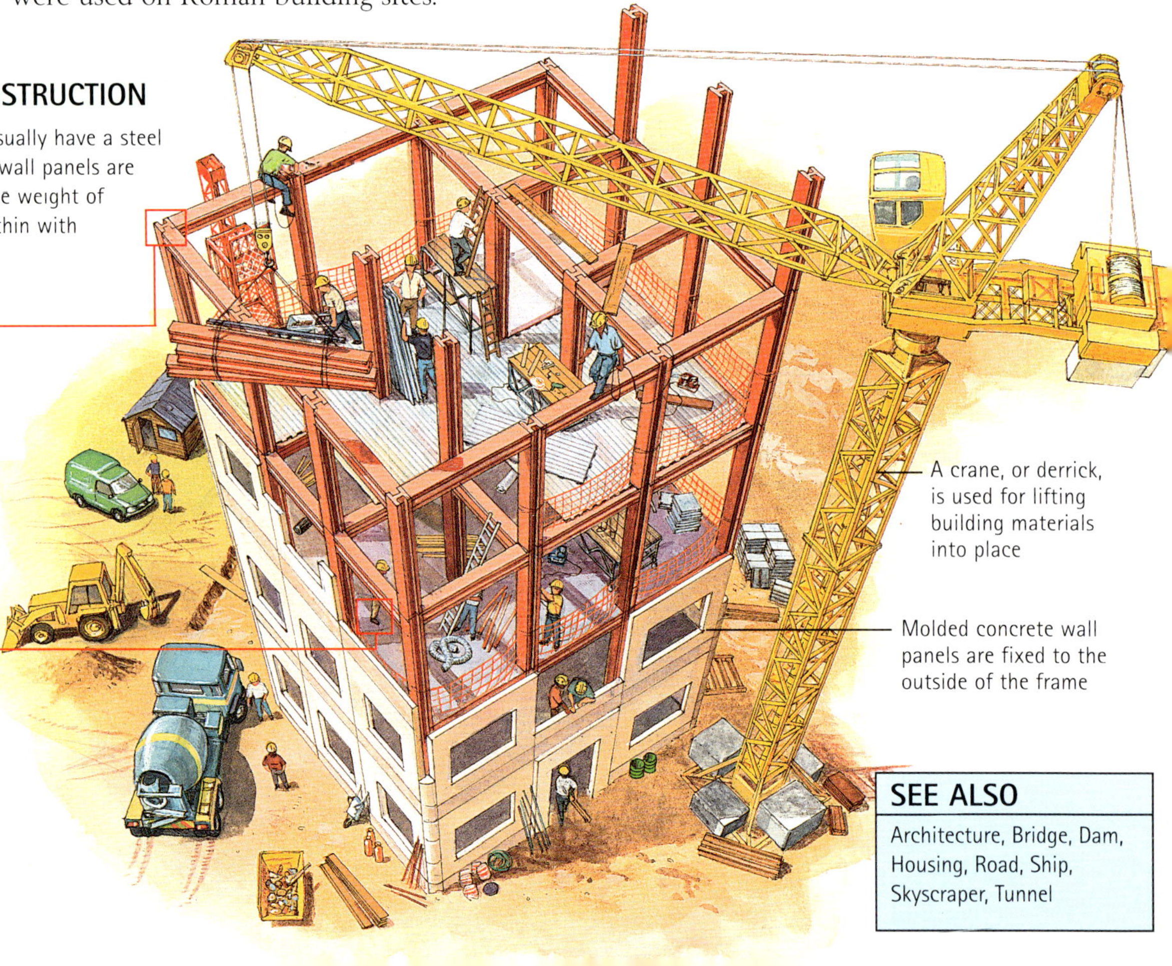

A crane, or derrick, is used for lifting building materials into place

Molded concrete wall panels are fixed to the outside of the frame

SEE ALSO

Architecture, Bridge, Dam, Housing, Road, Ship, Skyscraper, Tunnel

CONTINENT

Continents are large stretches of land unbroken by sea. There are seven continents on Earth.

HOW CONTINENTS DRIFT

All the land on Earth is fixed to giant plates which float on a sea of magma (melted rock). As the magma moves slowly, so do the continents, but some toward each other and others apart. Where two giant plates rub together, a crack sometimes appears in the Earth's surface, allowing magma to escape. Two such cracks, known as mid-ocean ridges, run through the Atlantic and Indian oceans.

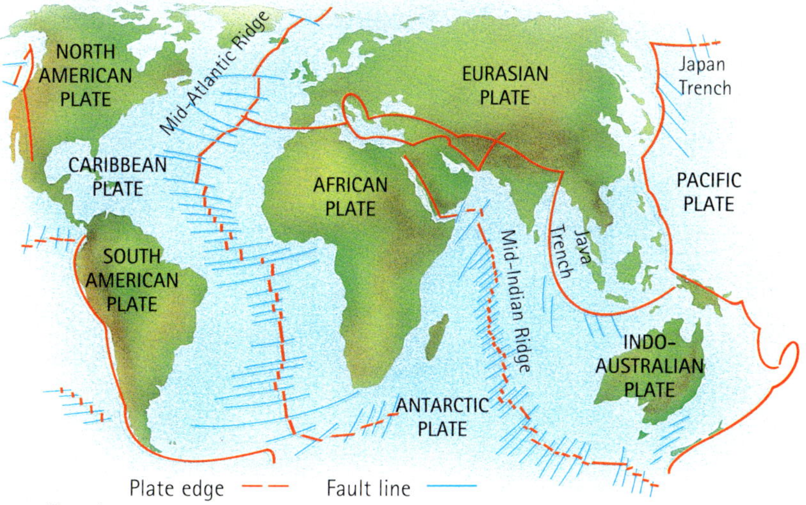

▲ The continents are attached to tectonic plates, the pieces that form the Earth's surface.

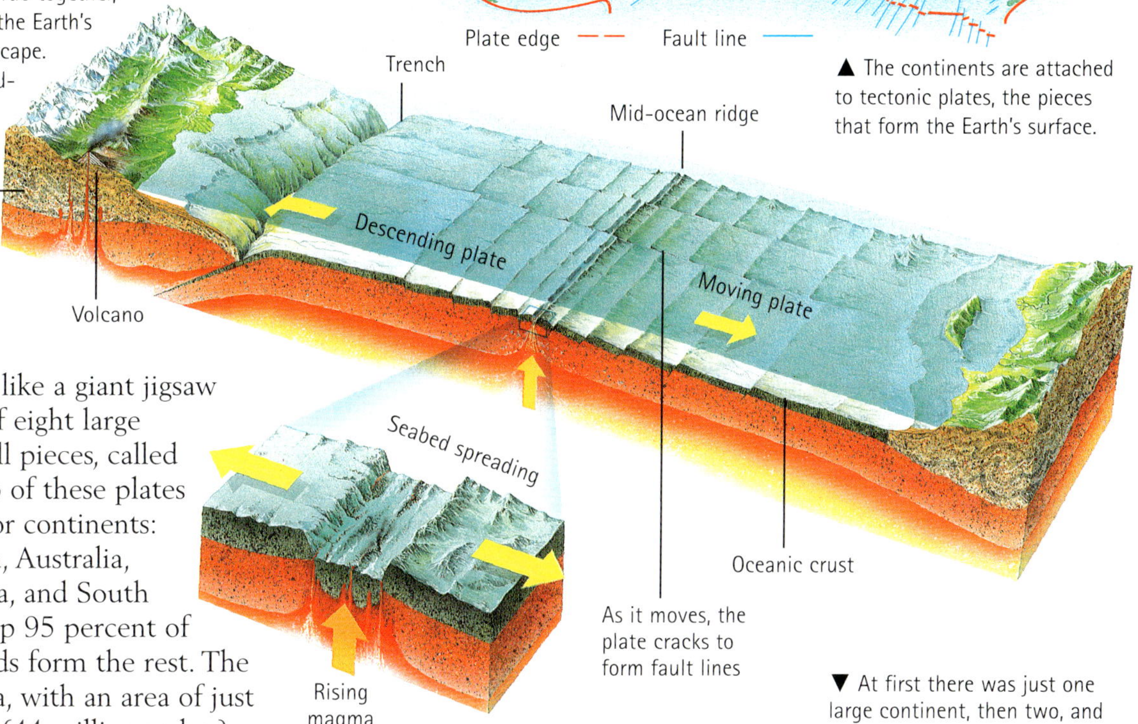

The Earth's crust is like a giant jigsaw puzzle made up of eight large pieces and several small pieces, called tectonic plates. On top of these plates sit seven land masses, or continents: Africa, Antarctica, Asia, Australia, Europe, North America, and South America. They make up 95 percent of Earth's land area; islands form the rest. The largest continent is Asia, with an area of just over 17 million sq. mi. (44 million sq km), and the smallest is Australia, covering about 3 million sq. mi. (7.7 million sq km).

CONTINENTAL CRUST

The continents are the thickest parts of the Earth's outer layer, or crust—in some places reaching down 38–45 mi. (60–70km). At the center, the continents contain the oldest rocks on the planet, with some dating back three billion years. As newer rocks were added around the fringes of these ancient cores, the continents grew.

FLOATING WORLD

The tectonic plates on which the continents sit are floating on a hot, molten layer called magma. Heat from deep inside the Earth keeps the magma moving slowly, and as it moves, so do the plates and continents. The slow movement of the continents is called continental drift.

VANISHED LANDS

More than 300 million years ago, all the land on Earth formed just one continent, called Pangaea. Then, about 180 million years ago, it split into two continents, called Gondwanaland and Laurasia. Slowly, North and South America broke away, India joined Asia, and Australia split from Antarctica and moved northward, until today's seven continents were created.

TOMORROW'S CONTINENTS

The movement is still continuing, and the continents we know today will look very different in 50 million years' time. Africa and the Americas, for example, will be even farther away from each other. North and South America will no longer be joined and Australia will have moved farther northward.

▼ At first there was just one large continent, then two, and finally the seven continents that we know were formed.

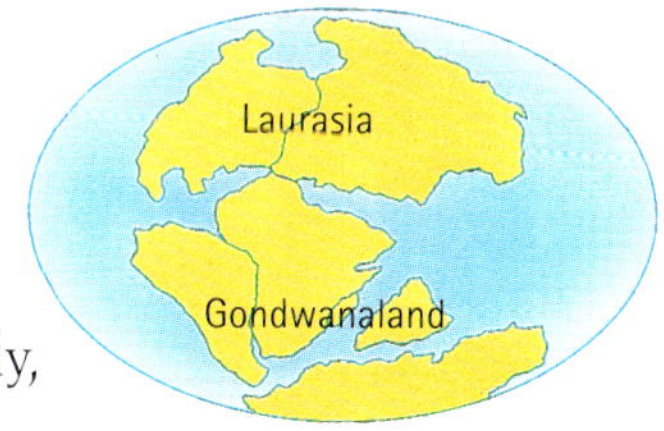

180 million years ago

65 million years ago

SEE ALSO

Africa, Antarctica, Asia, Australia, Earth, Europe, North America, Ocean and sea, South America

CRAB AND OTHER CRUSTACEANS

Crabs belong to a group of animals called crustaceans. These creatures have no bones and are covered with a hard shell called an exoskeleton.

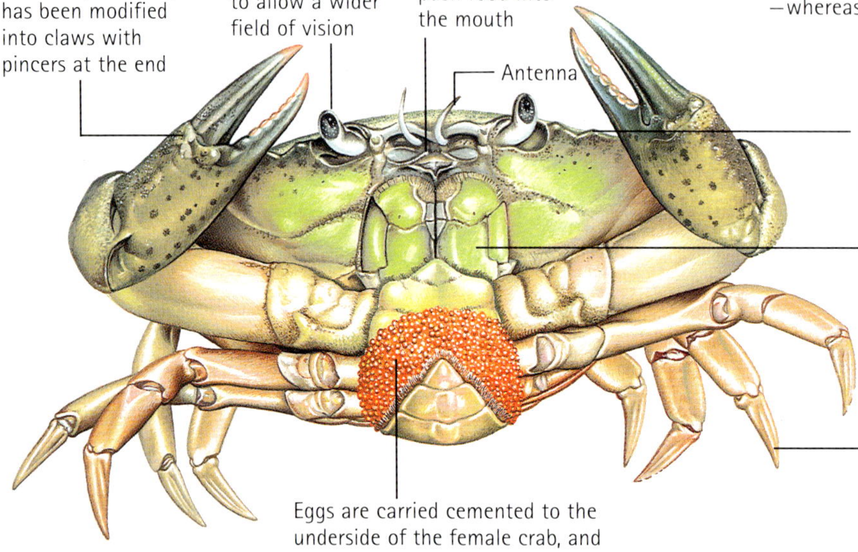

LIVING ON THE SHORELINE

Most crabs live in or near the sea, but many have adapted to life on land. The shore crab for instance, which spends most of its life out of water, has legs designed for walking —whereas swimming crabs have two paddle-shaped back legs.

The male fiddler crab has a very large claw, which it waves as part of a display to attract the female.

The hermit crab lives in an empty seashell, which it drags around with its two pairs of walking legs.

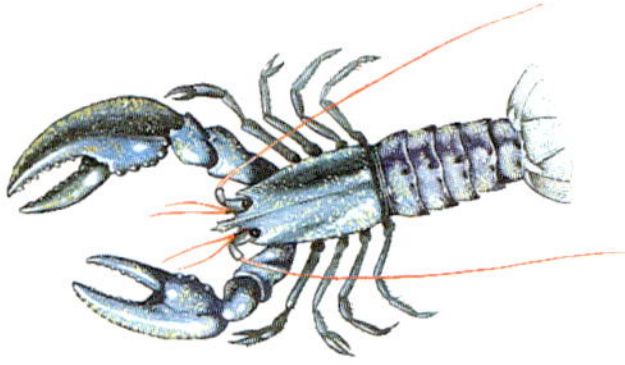

The lobster has one narrow claw for slicing dead fish, and a heavier claw for crushing clams.

The crayfish grows up to 16 in. (40cm) long. It lives in fresh water and has ten legs.

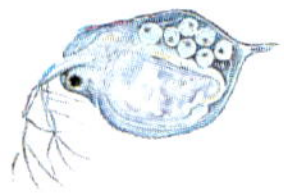

The water flea is one of the smallest crustaceans, growing to 0.008–0.7 in. (0.2–18mm) long.

The woodlouse is the only crustacean that lives entirely on land. It can roll itself up for defense.

Crustaceans include shrimps, lobsters, woodlice, water fleas, and barnacles. Altogether, there are about 42,000 species of crustaceans. Beneath its hard body shell, a crustacean's body is divided into sections, with jointed legs attached. Crabs, lobsters, and barnacles have especially thick shells, which contain a lot of chalklike material. This makes their shells feel like crusts.

EYES ON STALKS

There are about 4,500 species of crab. The smallest are the tiny pea crabs, which are less than 0.4 in. (1cm) across. The biggest are spider crabs, which live on the seabed and measure up to 13 ft. (4m) across from the tip of one leg to another. Crabs have ten legs, two of which are claws, and their eyes can move up and down on the end of stalks.

CRAB HABITS

Crabs usually live in water or close to the shore. Large crabs feed mainly on dead animals, which they tear up with their claws; small crabs pick up tiny scraps of food from the seabed. Many crabs move sideways on land. The robber crab climbs palm trees to pick young coconuts, which it bores into with its powerful claws.

WITHOUT A SHELL

A crab's body is armored by a shell which molts as the crab grows. The hermit crab, however, does not have a shell and must inhabit empty mollusk shells to protect its soft abdomen. As it grows, it searches for a larger shell to make its home.

HATCHED FROM EGGS

Crabs and other crustaceans reproduce by laying eggs. On hatching, the tiny larvae drift about in water, passing through several body changes before they become adults. In a few species, including the woodlouse, the young hatch out looking like mini-adults.

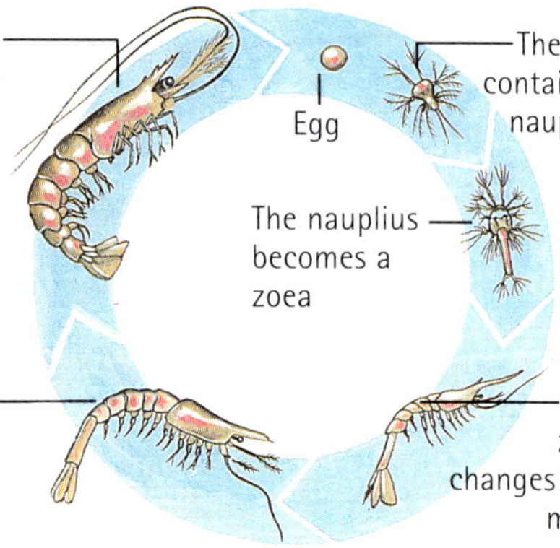

▲ A shrimp larva must pass through several stages before becoming an adult.

SEE ALSO
Animal, Seashore

Crop

Crops are plants that are grown to provide food for people and animals. They are also grown for useful materials like cotton and linen.

Wheat grows worldwide, in areas with moist, mild winters and dry summers.

Rice grows best in warm, wet areas such as China, where it is a staple food.

Potatoes came from Peru, but have long been an important crop in Europe.

Sugar beet is grown for its sugar-rich root. Its leaves are used as animal fodder.

Coffee is the major cash crop in tropical regions. It is grown on plantations.

Grapes are grown in vineyards and harvested for wine, raisins, and fresh fruit.

The type of crop grown by farmers depends on the climate of the country, the quality of the soil, and its demand in the market. In developing countries, especially in tropical parts of the world, people grow just enough of a crop for their own needs. These are called subsistence crops. Other people, usually farmers, grow large amounts of crops so that they can be sold. These are called cash crops.

ESSENTIAL CEREALS

The most important food crops are cereals—large grasses grown for their seeds or grains. Cereals include wheat, rice, corn, oats, sorghum, and millet, which cover about three fourths of the world's farmland. Wheat is the most popular cereal, with about 590 million tons grown every year, mainly for people to eat, but also as animal feed. Rice is the main ingredient in the diet of over half the world's people, particularly in Asia.

◀ Cotton is a cash crop. It is grown for its fibers, which are spun to make thread or fabric. Its seeds are also crushed to produce oil and fodder.

ROOTS TO FRUITS

Another vital food source is root crops—plants with edible fleshy roots. The potato is an important root crop in Europe, and yams and cassavas are staples in many parts of Africa. Cotton and flax are grown for their fibrous flowers, which are used to make cotton and linen. Other major crops include tea and tobacco, which are grown for their leaves, and fruits such as bananas and apples.

WILD ANCESTORS

All crops have come from wild plants, but they have been bred over time to provide bigger and better yields in soils or climates that are not their natural homes. Some crops have changed so much that it is hard to say which wild plants were their ancestors. As field and crop sizes have grown, the use of fertilizers, insecticides, and fungicides has also risen.

HARVESTING THE CROP

Combine harvesters automatically cut, thresh, and clean cereals such as wheat ready for transportation to market. Special attachments can be added to harvest different crops such as soybeans and corn.

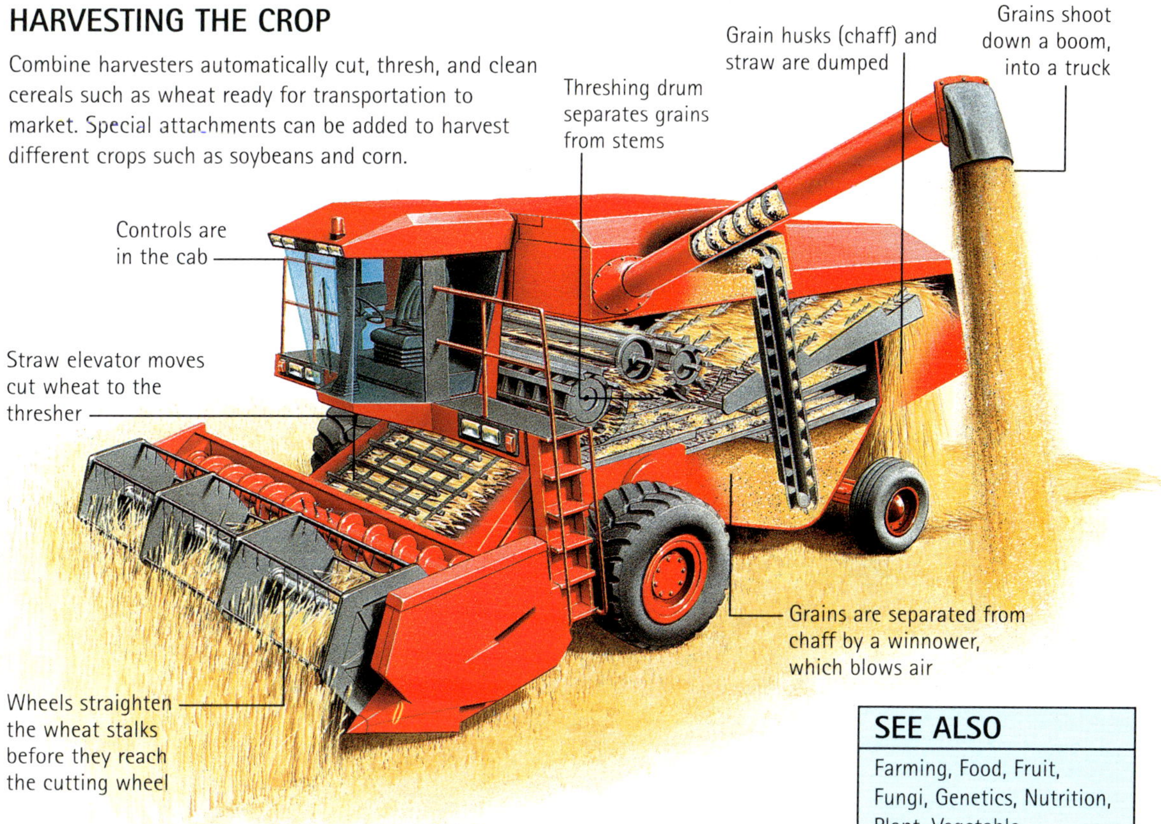

SEE ALSO

Farming, Food, Fruit, Fungi, Genetics, Nutrition, Plant, Vegetable

CRUSADES

The Crusades were a series of religious wars that took place in the Holy Land in the Middle Ages. They were fought between Christians and Muslims.

Nuredin was the Muslim leader who united the Islamic forces that Saladin took into battle at Hattin.

Sultan Saladin led the united Muslim armies and took Christian strongholds after the Second Crusade.

Louis IX ruled the coast around Acre, Syria for four years between the Seventh and Eighth Crusades.

For nearly 200 years, starting in 1096, Christians from Europe marched to Palestine to fight the Muslims for control of the Holy Land, especially of Jerusalem. They carried the Pope's blessing, but many fought for power and wealth.

THE BEGINNING

From the 600s, Muslim Arabs ruled the Holy Land, but Christian pilgrims were allowed to visit Jerusalem. Then, in 1071, the Muslim Turks captured Jerusalem and threatened the Christian Byzantine Empire. Pope Urban II called for Christian soldiers to unite and march to the Holy Land to recapture Jerusalem and protect pilgrims.

PILGRIM PEASANTS

The response to the Pope's call was vast. With cries of *Deus Vult!* (meaning "God wills it" in Latin), thousands of people began the long march eastward. The first to set out for the Byzantine capital of Constantinople were bands of poorly armed pilgrim peasants under the leadership of Peter the Hermit and Walter the Penniless. Many died on the way, and the rest were killed by the Muslims as soon as they reached Anatolia.

AN ARMY OF KNIGHTS

The First Crusade began in November 1096, when a large army, mostly of French and Norman knights under the leadership of noblemen such as Godfrey de Bouillon, gathered at Constantinople. It defeated the Muslims, capturing the cities of Antioch and Jerusalem, and set up a Christian kingdom along the Palestinian and Syrian coast.

JERUSALEM IS LOST

Muslim counterattacks started the Second Crusade (1147–49), in which King Louis VII of France and King Conrad II of Germany led separate attacks on Anatolia. These ended in failure for the Christians and weakened their hold on the Holy Land. In 1187, a new Muslim leader, Saladin, led Islamic opposition and wiped out the Crusaders at the Battle of the Horns of Hattin. He then captured Jerusalem and most of the Holy Land.

THE BATTLE OF ARSUF

In 1191, King Richard I secured victory over the Muslim leader Saladin at Arsuf, with a charge of armored knights. The charge was led by the Knights Templars and Knights Hospitallers—two military orders of skilled knights who were fanatical enemies of Islam and, like monks, took religious vows. Muslim troops, who wore only light armor, usually fled if they sensed defeat, but Richard lured them forward with defensive infantry tactics before unleashing his knights.

RICHARD THE LIONHEARTED

The Third Crusade (1189–92) was led by Richard I (Richard the Lionhearted of England), Frederick I of Germany, and Philip II of France. Unfortunately, Frederick drowned on the way, but the Crusaders defeated Saladin and retook much of the Holy Land, except Jerusalem.

LATER CRUSADES

The Fourth Crusade (1202–4) ended in chaos. Its leaders wanted power and riches, and concentrated on Constantinople instead of fighting for the Holy Land. The Christians then had little success in the Fifth Crusade (1217–21), but gained Jerusalem by treaty during the Sixth (1222–29). The Seventh Crusade (1248–54) ended with the capture of Louis IX of France, who was freed only after a ransom was paid.

FINAL BATTLE

During the Eighth Crusade (1270–72), the Muslims continued to advance. In 1291, they secured the last of the vital ports of Acre. No more Crusades took place and many of the knights retired to the island of Cyprus.

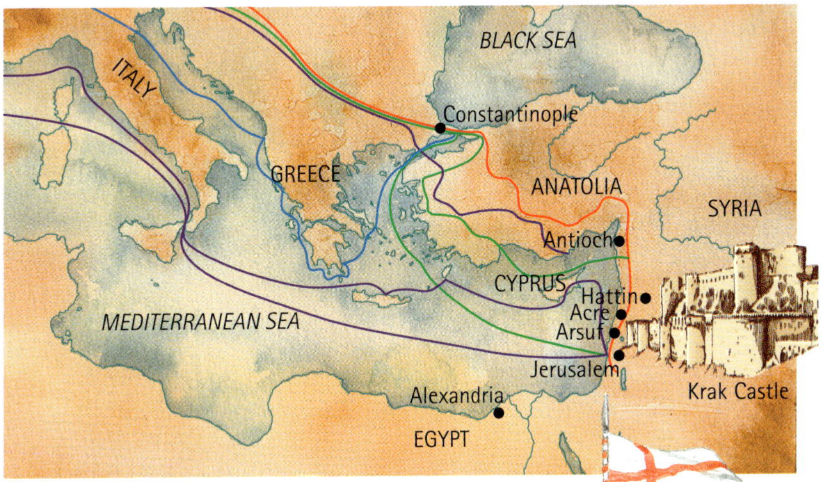

▲ The Crusaders traveled to the Holy Land by land and sea from all the Christian kingdoms of Europe. They built more than 100 castles and fortresses in the area. One of the best preserved is Krak des Chevaliers in Syria, which withstood 12 sieges before falling to the Muslims in 1271.

- First Crusade (1096–99)
- Second Crusade (1147–49)
- Third Crusade (1189–92)
- Fourth Crusade (1202–4)

King Richard I of England led the Third Crusade and was given the nickname of "Richard the Lionhearted."

SEE ALSO

Castle, Christianity, Empire, Islam, Middle Ages, Middle East, Warfare

CUSTOM

Customs are the traditions, rituals, and ways of behaving in a society that are passed on from generation to generation and are sometimes turned into laws.

Some Portuguese fishermen paint eyes on their boats to watch over them at sea and bring them back safely.

DANCING DRAGON

During the Chinese New Year festival, dancers inside a dragon costume move through the streets while firecrackers are set off. The dragon is believed to bring rain for a successful crop, and so has become a symbol of good fortune for the coming year. The firecrackers are to frighten away evil spirits.

The *haka*, performed by New Zealand rugby teams before a match, is based on a Maori war dance.

The custom of carving pumpkin faces comes from the Celtic Day of the Dead, celebrated on October 31.

The *chanoyu*, a Japanese tea ceremony which can last for four hours, came originally from China.

The painting of eggs is a symbol of new life which has been adopted by Christians at Easter.

Every society has its own customs, waiting politely in line, for example, or wearing a particular costume during a celebration. Learning about different customs helps us to understand people from other countries or cultures.

RITES OF PASSAGE

Across the world, customs are different, but there are times of life, known as rites of passage, when a person's status changes. Such times include birth, coming of age, marriage, and death—occasions that are marked by elaborate customs in every society. The custom of keeping mother and baby secluded from society for a month after birth is a common custom in many countries, probably based on fear of infection. There are also many customs marking a young person's move from childhood to adulthood, ranging from throwing a party to a religious ritual.

LINKS WITH THE PAST

Customs may be adapted over time, often as a result of industrialization or contact with other cultures. A custom's original meaning may be forgotten, or it may continue as a way of keeping a link with the past. The special Thanksgiving meal, for example, is usually celebrated with the whole family and commemorates the survival of Pilgrim families long ago.

CUSTOMARY GREETINGS

Everyday customs help people to bond with other members of their society. For instance, every culture has a customary way of greeting—Europeans kiss or shake hands, the Inuit rub noses, and the Chinese bow. By taking part in customs, people demonstrate their membership of a group or society.

GOING AGAINST THE GRAIN

Refusing to follow a custom can offend; it may even lead to the exclusion of an individual from a group of society. Customs are not laws, but because they are designed to help us understand what is acceptable behavior in a society, customs are often included in laws or religious codes.

▲ In Hindu weddings, everything is brightly colored, and the bride usually wears a red sari with lots of gold jewelry.

SEE ALSO

Clothing, Dance, Food, Judaism

DAM

A dam is a barrier built across a river or stream to hold back water. The stored water may be used for irrigation, as drinking water, or to provide power.

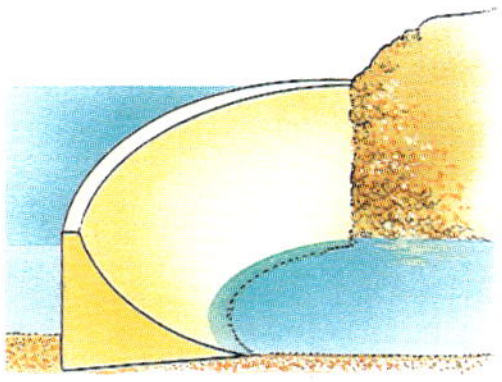

Arch dams, used in tall, narrow canyons or gorges, are often surprisingly thin.

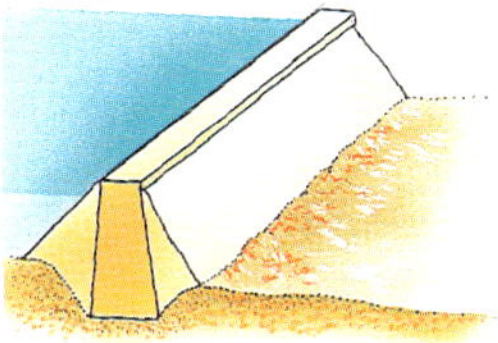

Concrete gravity dams are built to hold back water in broad, shallow valleys.

Embankment dams have a reinforced inner wall to hold back shallow lakes.

The earliest dams were built in the Middle East about 5,000 years ago. These dams were used to direct water to fields of crops, through canals called irrigation channels. A dam built on the Orontes River in Syria about 1300 B.C. still irrigates fields near the city of Homs.

CONTROLLING THE FLOW

Today, dams are still built for irrigation, as well as to stop flooding and to provide water power for electricity. In low-lying areas of China, Bangladesh, and the United States, dams have been built to stop flood disasters. Other dams are built so that water can be stored in artificial lakes, or reservoirs. The water is then supplied to homes and industry.

HYDROELECTRIC DAM

Hydroelectric dams use water power to produce electricity. They require large quantities of water and a very long drop from the top to the bottom of the dam. About 20 percent of the world's electricity is generated by hydroelectric dams.

1 Water from the reservoir passes through a gate.

2 The flow of the water turns wheels (turbines).

3 The turbines turn dynamos to create electricity.

4 Cables carry the electricity away.

5 Excess water flows over a sluice.

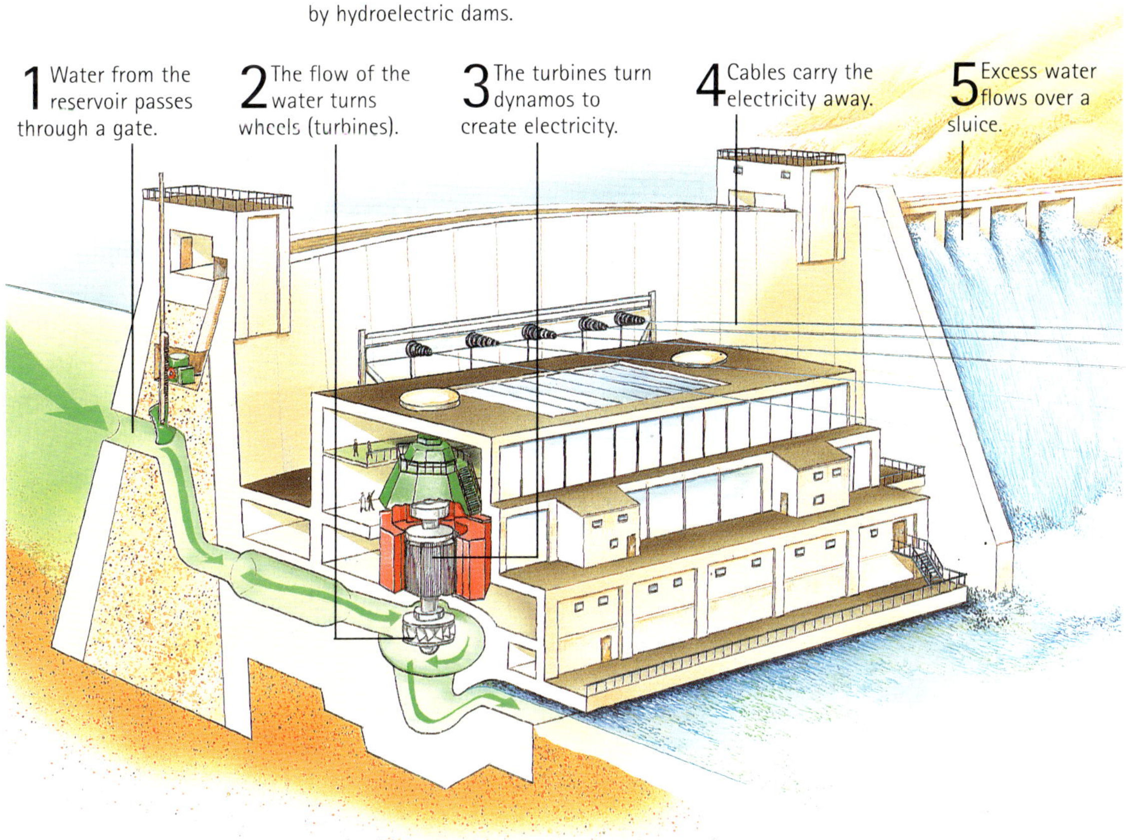

EMBANKMENT DAMS

The simplest dams are embankment dams. They are made from earth and rock and have a waterproof core to stop water seeping through. The Aswan High Dam in Egypt controls the annual flooding of the Nile River and provides hydroelectric power for the whole country.

GRAVITY AND ARCH

Gravity dams are made of stone or concrete. They rely on their weight and strength to hold back the water. Arch dams are curved so that the weight of the water is pushed out from the dam to the canyon or gorge. They can be very thin—for example, the Vaiont Dam in the Italian Alps is 870 ft. (265m) high but only 75.5 ft. (23m) thick at its base.

ENVIRONMENTAL IMPACT

Dam building affects the surrounding environment, and wildlife can be destroyed. Some dams have fish ladders, which enable fish such as salmon to make their journey upstream to breed.

FAST FACTS

- The world's largest dam is the Syncrude Tailings Dam in Alberta, Canada
- At 551 ft. (168m), the Grand Coulee Dam, in the state of Washington, is 200 ft. (20m) taller than the Great Pyramid in Egypt
- Dams were so important in ancient Mesopotamia that King Hammurabi's laws said that anyone who broke a dam should be sold into slavery to pay the farmer

SEE ALSO

Construction, Egypt, Waterpower

Dance

Dance is one of the oldest art forms. It is the rhythmic movement of all or part of the body, and includes ballet, the waltz, flamenco, tap, rumba, and disco.

Dancing can express emotion,tell a story, create a specific atmosphere, or show off physical strength. There are two main types of dance: social dancing for enjoyment, and dance created to entertain an audience.

DANCING THROUGH HISTORY

People have been dancing for thousands of years—dancing figures appear in cave paintings in Europe and Africa dating back to prehistoric times. Many of the earliest dances that are still popular today were connected with religious ceremonies or superstitious beliefs. English morris dancing is based on ancient war rituals, and voodoo dancers in Haiti go into a trance in which they attempt to summon the spirits. The expressive dance drama of the Ancient Greeks has had a long-lasting influence in the West.

► Ice-skating competitions feature ice dancing in their freestyle section. Couples are not allowed to lift one another, but often imitate traditional ballroom dance routines using daring athletic poses.

GETTING TOGETHER

Formal social dances, where set steps are followed, go back many centuries. Bugaku dancing in Japan originated in the A.D. 600s. In medieval Europe, grand social dances were popular at court. Most were adapted from the simple country dances of ordinary people. As early as the 1400s, there were dance teachers who taught the steps to the latest dances.

CLASSIC BEAUTY

Ballet originated in the royal courts of Italy during the 1400s, but was developed in France. King Louis XIV was an enthusiastic dancer, and opened the first European dance academy in Paris in 1661. Until then, most dancers had been amateur, but professional dancers soon began to appear. The academy's director, Charles-Louis Beauchamp, helped to standardize the classic movements. He is thought to have set out the five basic ballet positions of the feet and arms. By the mid-1800s, romantic ballets such as *La Sylphide* were popular in Europe.

▲ Music and dance are important in the cultures of many tribal countries, such as Zimbabwe, Africa. Here a Shangaan dancer, in an elaborate costume with wings, mask, and grass skirt, performs a tribal dance.

▲ Ballet tells a story, whether it is a classical tale such as *Swan Lake*, or a favorite children's story like *Alice in Wonderland*. Here, during her journey through Wonderland, Alice (far right) meets the fearsome Queen of Hearts (in white skirt with red hearts).

▲ Dancing to repetitive music with a powerful underlying beat, often in strobe lighting, swept clubs in the 1990s.

▼ In the popular Japanese theater of Kabuki, an all-male cast performs comic dance, drama, and singing shows, often in female dress. To give a visual climax, each scene ends with a pose called the *mie*.

▲ Contemporary dance is less structured than ballet and does not always tell a story. It often uses choreography (arrangement) of the dancers' bodies to form striking poses.

BREAKING AWAY

The second half of the 1800s was the era of classical Russian ballet, with great masterpieces such as Tchaikovsky's *Swan Lake*. But by the early 1900s, some dancers were beginning to create a freer style, breaking away from the rigid patterns and training of classical ballet. The American dancer Isadora Duncan was a big influence on contemporary dance. She performed barefoot, basing her moves on ideas inspired by Ancient Greece.

TAKE YOUR PARTNERS

As time went by, trends in social dances changed along with styles of music. In the 1800s, the waltz caused a scandal because the man and woman dancing held each other so close. Exciting new dances in the 1900s were based partly on African-American and Irish traditions, like jazz and tap. In the 1920s, while dramatic Russian ballets toured Europe, people in the United States were dancing the high-kicking Charleston.

DANCE FADS

Jitterbugging became popular in the 1930s and 1940s, and developed into the sensational rock'n'roll jive of the 1940s and 1950s. The twist was a popular dance in the 1960s, and the latter part of the 1900s has been marked by disco, breakdancing, and free expression.

SEE ALSO

Africa, Custom, Music, Theater

DEMOCRACY

Democracy is a form of government in which the people take part in ruling the state. The people may rule directly or through elected officials.

◀ Two metal voting disks were given to each man in ancient Athens. They were used in criminal trials to vote guilty or not guilty.

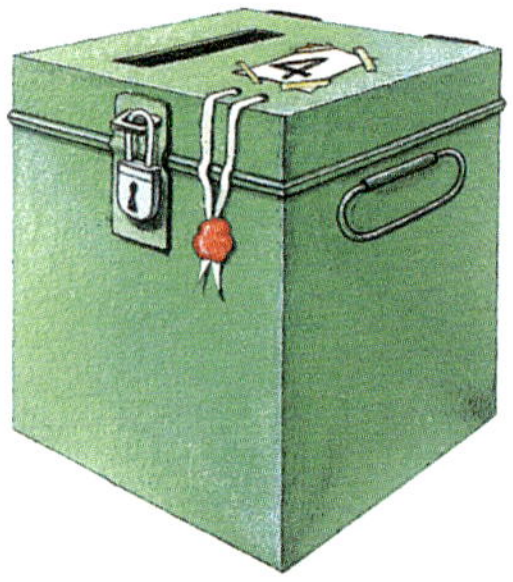

◀ In some elections, a person votes by making a mark next to the candidate's name on a ballot paper. The papers (votes) are posted in a sealed ballot box, to be counted later.

FAST FACTS

- In Ancient Greece, women, children, slaves, and foreigners (about 90 percent of the people) could not vote
- In many towns in New England, everyone votes on laws directly, in a town meeting
- Judges or independent officials make sure the government obeys the law in most democracies

People who live in a democracy either vote for officials who make laws for them, or they vote directly on laws in a meeting known as an assembly. Democracy allows people freedom of speech and the right to choose between competing political parties in regularly held elections.

POWER TO THE PEOPLE

The first democracy appeared in Ancient Greece in the 500s B.C., when men in cities could vote in assemblies. The word democracy is Greek for "rule by the people."

ELECTION VICTORY

India is the world's largest democracy, and election time plays an important part in the lives of the people. Candidates make speeches, distribute leaflets, advertise, and design posters to persuade people to vote for them. Most candidates belong to a political party whose members share the same ideas about how the country should be run.

ELECTED ASSEMBLIES

The reign of Alexander the Great and a succession of Roman emperors gradually put an end to democracy, and the Middle Ages saw the rise of feudalism and monarchy. Democracy reappeared in the 1600s, when elected assemblies began to take power in some countries. At first only wealthy men could vote, but today nearly every adult in a democracy is allowed to vote.

MAJORITY RULE

Voters choose people to represent them in legislatures (lawmaking bodies), such as the U.S. Senate or the House of Representatives. For a law to be passed, a majority in the legislature must vote for it. On important issues, there may be a vote of all the people: a referendum.

CHOOSING REPRESENTATIVES

Some elections are decided by a system in which the candidate with the most votes wins. Others are decided by proportional representation—each party gets candidates in parliament in relation to the number of votes it receives.

GOVERNMENTS AND THE LAW

There are many kinds of democracy. In Britain, there is a monarchy, but an elected parliament makes laws. France is a republic with a president and prime minister, as well as a legislature. Many former Soviet Union and Eastern European nations are becoming increasingly democratic since the fall of their communist governments.

SEE ALSO

Civil rights, Government, Greece (Ancient), Law, Politics

Desert

Deserts are dry areas of land which have hardly any plants or animals. Most deserts are hot, get very little rain, and are sandy or rocky.

▲ Deserts are not always hot. Some places in Antarctica and Greenland are known as polar deserts because the ground there is so dry. For example, on the western side of Antarctica, there are areas that receive less than 5 in. (13cm) of snow each year.

More than a fifth of the world's land is so dry that it is known as desert. Most deserts receive less than 10 in. (250mm) of rain each year. Others receive more rain, but it quickly evaporates in the strong heat and winds, or sinks into the parched ground. The driest place in the world is Chile's Atacama Desert, parts of which have less than 0.004 in. (0.1mm) of rain each year.

WHERE DESERTS FORM

Most deserts, such as the Kalahari and Sahara in Africa, lie between the Tropic of Cancer and the Tropic of Capricorn (25° to the north and south of the equator). These are the tropics, where the air is often too hot and dry for rain clouds to form. The cold Gobi Desert in central Asia exists, however, because it is far from the sea's moist winds. Other deserts, like the Atacama, lie behind high mountains which block rain-bearing winds.

SURVIVAL TACTICS

Desert plants and animals have developed ways of coping with the lack of water. Plants usually have long, spreading roots to reach any available moisture. Most have spines or small leaves that are rolled or waxy to cut down on water loss through evaporation. Other plants spend most of their lives as seeds—only growing when rain falls. Desert animals often hide during the heat of the day and come out at night. Camels can go for many days without water.

POCKETS OF WATER

Oases are pockets of fertile land in a desert. These occur where an aquifer, or underground stream, comes to the surface. Plants such as palm trees thrive, and animals and people gather there.

CREEPING DESERTS

Deserts can spread. This may happen because the climate becomes drier or nearby land is overgrazed by farm animals.

IN THE SHADOW OF THE SIERRA NEVADA

The deserts of North America are shielded from rain by the towering mountain wall of the Sierra Nevada. In some areas, less than 4 in. (100mm) of rain falls, making the gravelly ground inhospitable except to a few plants and animals. Temperatures during the day can reach 212°F (100°C), but at night it is often near freezing because there is no cloud cover.

With its shallow, wide-ranging roots, the saguaro cactus always finds water

Some honeypot ants fill themselves with liquid, and act as reservoirs for the rest of the nest

Scaly skin stops the rattlesnake from drying out

The kit fox sleeps in a cool burrow during the day

The roadrunner gets most of its water from the animals it catches

The prickly pear cactus stores water in its fleshy stem

SEE ALSO

Africa, Antarctica, Climate, Habitat, Plant, South America

Design

Everything we use today, from a toothbrush to a car, has been designed according to its function, trends in fashion and art, and the latest available materials.

Spanish painter Salvador Dali designed this "Eye of Time" watch.

Even household appliances, such as the kettle, are always being redesigned.

Scottish designer and architect Charles Rennie Mackintosh designed all his chairs with unusually high backs.

Professional designers must create an object that does the job it is supposed to do as efficiently as possible. But they must also think carefully about the aesthetic value, or appearance, of the object, how and where it will be used, who will be using it, and changing trends in technology and materials.

AGE OF DESIGN

The word design comes from the Italian word *disegno*. From the 1300s to the mid-1500s, during the great Italian artistic era called the Renaissance, the word was used to describe the basic idea behind a work of art, as well as rough sketches of it. Today, the term covers a huge area, from detailed drawings and engineering plans for buildings to the graphic design of books, magazines, and product containers.

SKETCHING IT OUT

The first step for many designers, whether painters, architects, film set designers, or fashion designers, is to sketch out their ideas, or create storyboards on paper. If it is a building or product, they may then make up a small model to scale. Fashion designers often make up a sample garment, using inexpensive cloth.

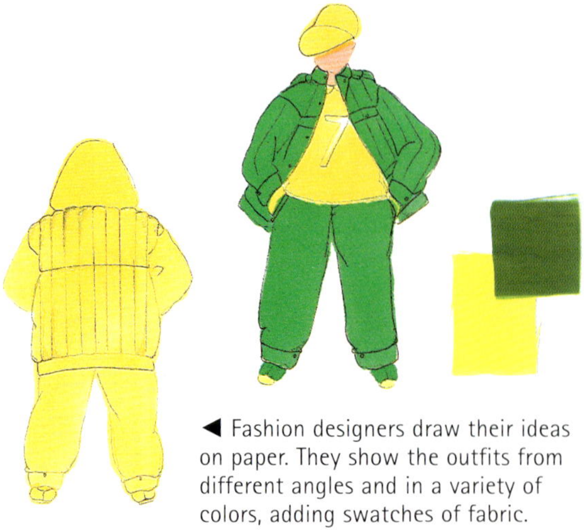

◀ Fashion designers draw their ideas on paper. They show the outfits from different angles and in a variety of colors, adding swatches of fabric.

DESIGNING ON COMPUTERS

Computers are now used extensively in design, especially for industry. They allow people to experiment with three-dimensional, often animated, models on the screen. Using CAD (computer-aided design), a designer can quickly change a detail and the computer will calculate and apply the changes to the rest of the design. Specialist programs help experts create cars, shoes, and electrical goods.

THE CREATIVE PROCESS

Computers can be used to highlight stress points, illustrate aerodynamics, and show other crucial design features of a prototype car. Newspapers and magazines are designed on computers, as was this book.

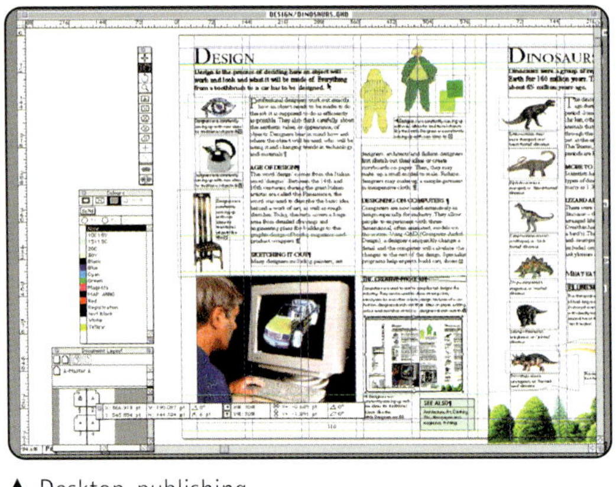

▲ Desktop-publishing software has revolutionized page design—changes can now be made in seconds.

SEE ALSO

Architecture, Art, Clothing, Computer

DINOSAUR

Dinosaurs were a type of reptile that lived on Earth for over 160 million years. They became extinct about 65 million years ago.

Tyrannosaurus rex was a theropod, or "beast-footed" dinosaur.

Diplodocus was a sauropod, or "lizard-footed" dinosaur.

Camptosaurus was an ornithopod, or "bird-footed" dinosaur.

Stegosaurus was a stegosaur, or "roofed" dinosaur.

Sauropelta was an ankylosaur, or "jointed" dinosaur.

Triceratops was a ceratopsian, or "horned-head" dinosaur.

The dinosaurs evolved 225 million years ago during a geological period known as the Triassic. Some were only the size of a chicken, others were the largest land animals that ever existed. They roamed the planet throughout the Jurassic period and died out at the end of the Cretaceous period. The Triassic, Jurassic, and Cretaceous periods are known as the "age of reptiles."

MORE TO COME

The same dinosaurs did not exist throughout the age of reptiles. For example, *Diplodocus* lived during the Jurassic and *Tyrannosaurus* reigned in the Cretaceous period. Scientists have found evidence of over 500 types of dinosaur, spanning all the periods, but it is believed that as many as 1,300 types may have existed—most of which are still undiscovered.

LIZARD OR BIRDLIKE

There were two main groups, or orders, of dinosaur—the Saurischia (with hipbones arranged like a lizard's) and the Ornithischia (with hipbones arranged like a bird's). The Saurischia can be divided into two smaller groups known as the theropods and the sauropods. The Ornithischia include four groups: the ornithopods, the stegosaurs, the ankylosaurs, and the ceratopsians.

MEAT-EATERS

The theropods were meat-eaters, all built to the same design. They had long mouths full of teeth for tearing flesh, they walked on their hind legs, and had small bodies which they balanced with long, heavy tails. Some, such as *Compsognathus*, were chicken-size, while the biggest were 39.4 ft. (12m)-long killers, such as *Tyrannosaurus*. ▶

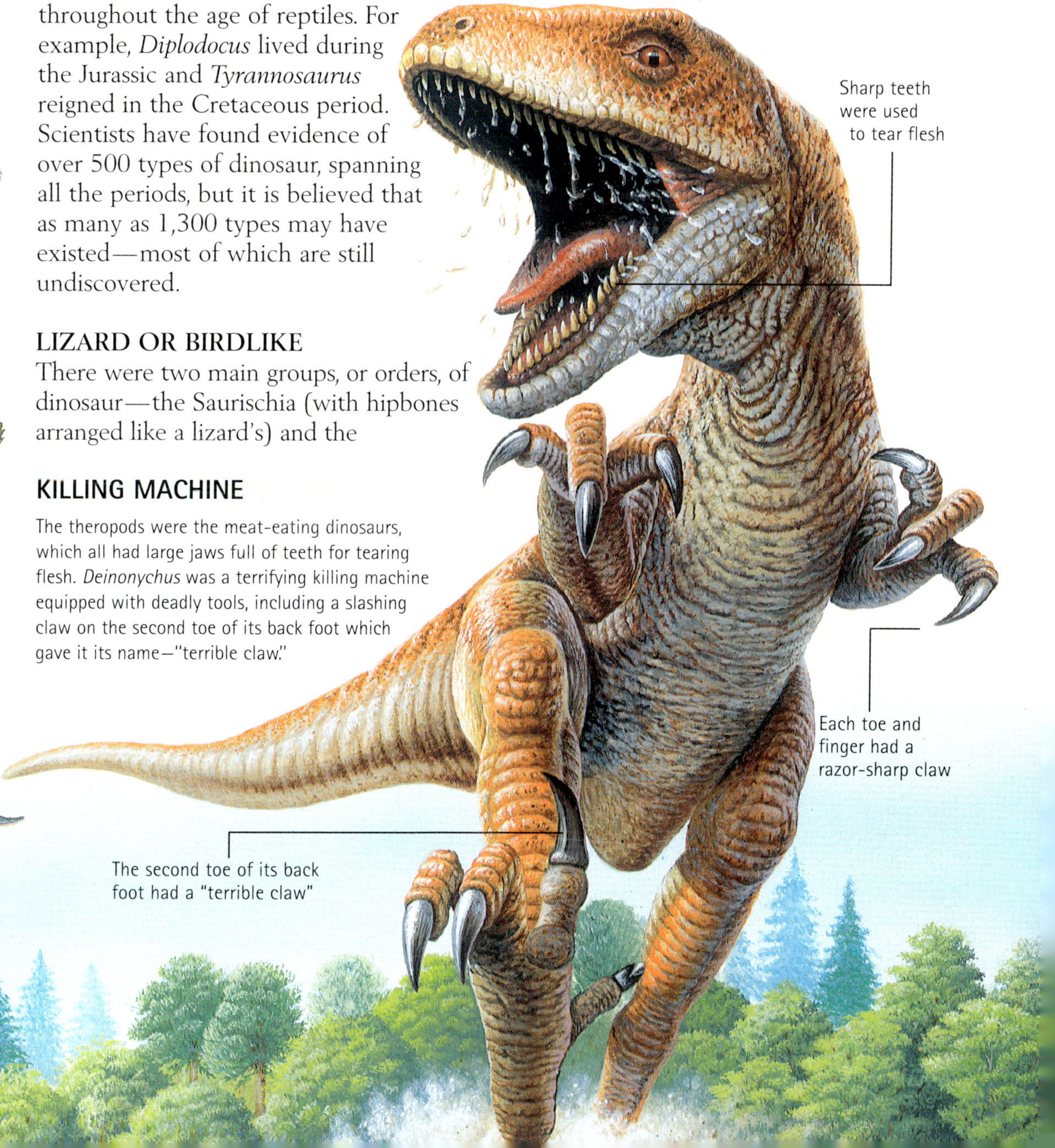

KILLING MACHINE

The theropods were the meat-eating dinosaurs, which all had large jaws full of teeth for tearing flesh. *Deinonychus* was a terrifying killing machine equipped with deadly tools, including a slashing claw on the second toe of its back foot which gave it its name—"terrible claw."

▲ A comparison between the size of mighty *Tyrannosaurus*'s feet and those of an average man.

DINOSAUR GIANTS

Sauropods were plant-eaters. They had large, heavy bodies and moved around on all fours, using their long necks to reach leaves on trees. They were the largest land animals that ever lived and included *Diplodocus* and *Brachiosaurus*.

PLANT-EATERS

The Ornithischia dinosaurs were also all plant-eaters. The only ones that could walk on their hind legs were the ornithopods. They had a more sophisticated chewing system than the long-necked sauropods, with cheeks for holding the food while they chewed it. *Iguanodon* is probably the most famous of the ornithopods.

▲ In 1978, a fossilized nest of 15 young *Maiasaura* was found in Montana. Evidence showed that the young were very small and would have had to be cared for by the mother to survive. *Maiasaura* means "good mother lizard."

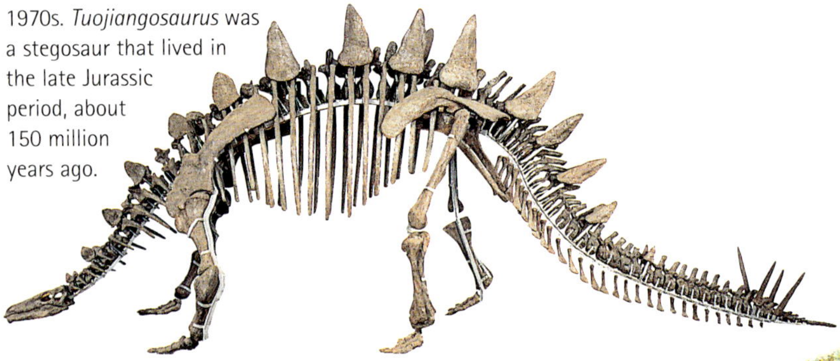

▼ This fossil skeleton of *Tuojiangosaurus* was discovered in China in the 1970s. *Tuojiangosaurus* was a stegosaur that lived in the late Jurassic period, about 150 million years ago.

BONY ARMOR

Three ornithischian groups evolved from the ornithopods (bird-footed dinosaurs). They all had armor of some kind that made them heavy, so they walked on four legs. The first was the stegosaurs—the "roofed" dinosaurs. They had large bodies and either a double row of bony plates down the back like *Stegosaurus*, or an arrangement of spines like *Kentrosaurus*.

A SCENE FROM THE LATE JURASSIC

The late Jurassic is the period from 157 to 145 million years ago. It is known for its many plant-eating dinosaur species, such as spiny *Stegosaurus* and long-necked sauropods, including *Apatosaurus*. The main dinosaur predator was the meat-eating *Allosaurus*, but the reptile *Diplosaurus*, an ancestor of the crocodile, was also frightening.

A SCENE FROM THE LATE CRETACEOUS

The Late Cretaceous was a period from 95 to 65 million years ago. It was dominated by herds of duckbilled *Edmontosaura*, which had replaced the sauropods as the main plant-eaters. Meat-eating *Tyrannosaurus* probably hunted these animals, because other plant-eaters like *Triceratops* and *Ankylosaurus* had developed spectacular defensive armor. Large flying reptiles may have scavenged like vultures on the bodies of dead dinosaurs.

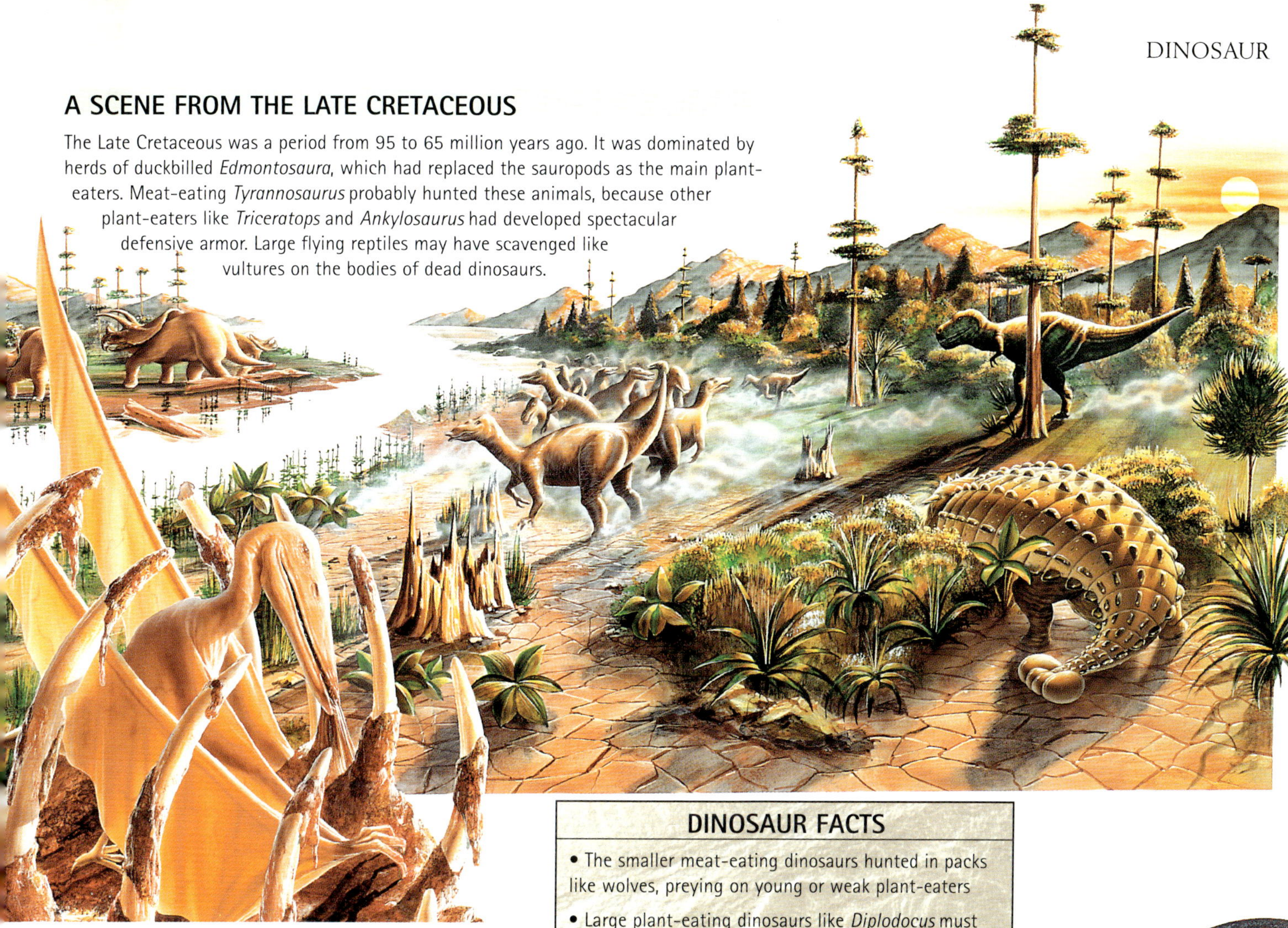

DINOSAUR FACTS

- The smaller meat-eating dinosaurs hunted in packs like wolves, preying on young or weak plant-eaters
- Large plant-eating dinosaurs like *Diplodocus* must have had to eat continuously to avoid starvation
- Dinosaurs may have been warm-blooded like mammals and birds
- Many different types of insect and mammal also lived during the time of the dinosaurs
- The dinosaurs' legs were not at the side like reptiles', but under their bodies like mammals'

JOINTED DINOSAURS

The second ornithischian group was the ankylosaurs, or "jointed" dinosaurs. They had bony armor that lay flat over their broad backs, and were also armed with spikes along the sides, as in *Edmontonia*, or a tail with a club, as in *Euoplocephalus*.

HORNED HEADS

The last ornithiscian group was the ceratopsians. They had armor on their faces and heads, where it formed big bony frills around the neck. These "horned-head" dinosaurs included *Triceratops*, which had a small horn on the nose and two long horns over the eyes, and *Styracosaurus*, which had an enormous horn on the nose and a series of smaller horns around the frill.

REPTILE NEIGHBORS

Dinosaurs were not the only reptiles that lived at the time. Many groups of swimming reptiles, such as the fish-shaped ichthyosaurs and the long-necked plesiosaurs, lived in the sea; pterosaurs flew in the air.

DEATH OF THE REPTILES

All of these unusual reptiles became extinct along with the dinosaurs at the end of the Cretaceous period. No one knows for sure how this happened, or why other reptiles, such as crocodiles and turtles, survived. It may have been a gradual process, due to a slow climatic change, or there may have been a sudden catastrophe, such as the Earth's being hit by a gigantic meteorite. The dinosaurs did leave some relatives, however. During the Jurassic period, birds evolved from the small meat-eating theropods, which means today's birds are the direct descendants of the dinosaurs.

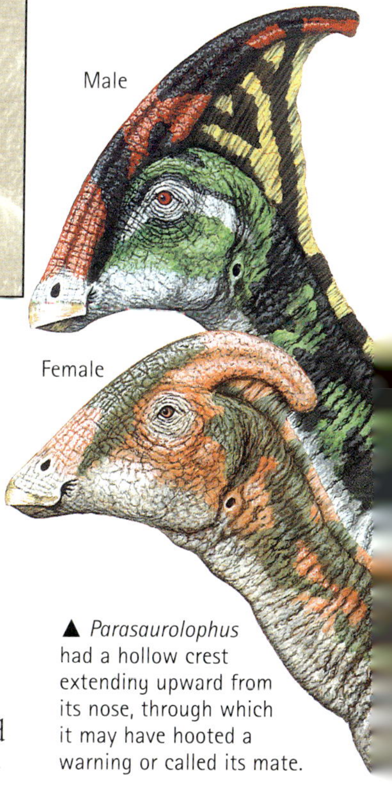

▲ *Parasaurolophus* had a hollow crest extending upward from its nose, through which it may have hooted a warning or called its mate.

SEE ALSO

Evolution, Fossil, Mammal, Prehistoric animal, Reptile

DISEASE

A disease is an illness that disturbs the normal healthy functioning of a plant, animal, or person. Each disease produces symptoms (physical changes).

The human body may be attacked by thousands of diseases. These range from relatively harmless ones, such as the common cold and athlete's foot, to life-threatening diseases, such as typhoid and some cancers. Plants and animals also suffer from diseases—potatoes suffer from blight, and cats can get the flu (influenza).

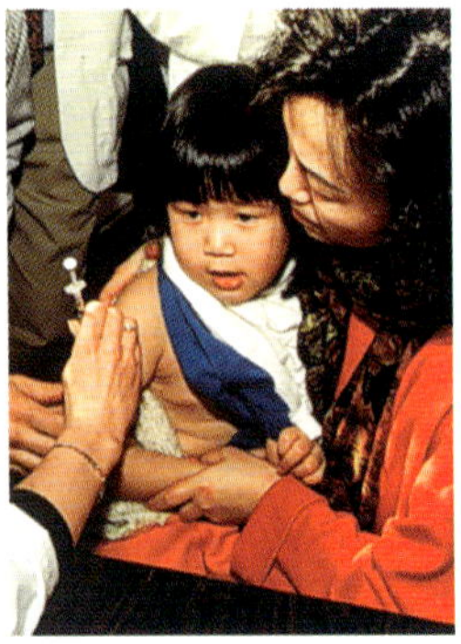

▲ Many diseases have almost been wiped out by the widespread use of inoculation (also called immunization and vaccination). This is when a milder form of the disease is introduced into the body, by injection or via the mouth, so that the person develops long-term resistance to the disease.

BACTERIA AND VIRUSES

Flu, AIDS, and tetanus are all infectious diseases. They are caused by harmful microscopic organisms we call germs that invade the body and multiply. Tetanus is caused by bacteria (living creatures); flu and AIDS are caused by viruses (bundles of DNA wrapped in protein). Infectious diseases are spread from person to person by, for example, breathing in germs. A sudden outbreak of an infectious disease which affects many people is called an epidemic. Some infectious diseases can be prevented with vaccinations, and others can be treated with medicines such as antibiotics.

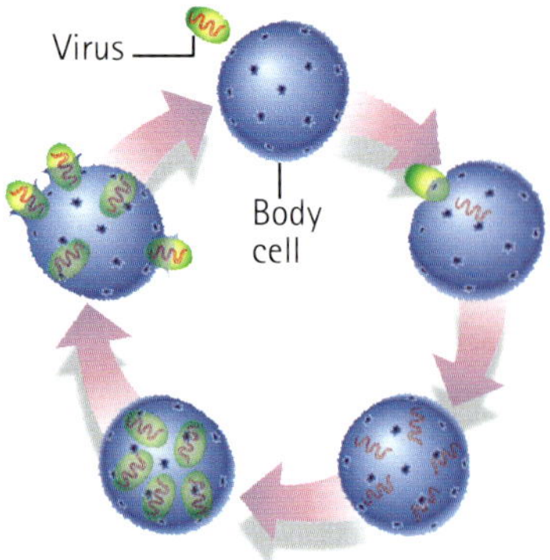

VIRUS ATTACK
A virus spreads in the body by using the body's cells to make copies of itself. As the replicas break out, they destroy the body's cell, and each virus starts the process again.

NONINFECTIOUS DISEASES

Many diseases are not caused by germs, but are the result of a poor diet. An example of this is scurvy, which is the result of not eating enough vitamin C. Others may be caused by an unhealthy lifestyle. For example, smoking and stress can lead to heart disease. Some diseases, such as hemophilia, run in families as a result of faulty genes.

LOOKING FOR CLUES

Symptoms such as pain or fever tell the person suffering from a disease that something is wrong, and give clues to doctors as to the cause. A doctor can also detect signs of disease by taking X rays or blood tests.

AFRICAN SLEEPING SICKNESS

In some areas of Africa, the tsetse fly spreads a disease called sleeping sickness. When it feeds on human blood, this tiny fly injects some of its saliva into the person's bloodstream. If its saliva contains microorganisms called *Trypanosoma brucci*, these enter the bloodstream also, and multiply inside the body, causing fever, headaches, and sleepiness. The person may die if not treated quickly.

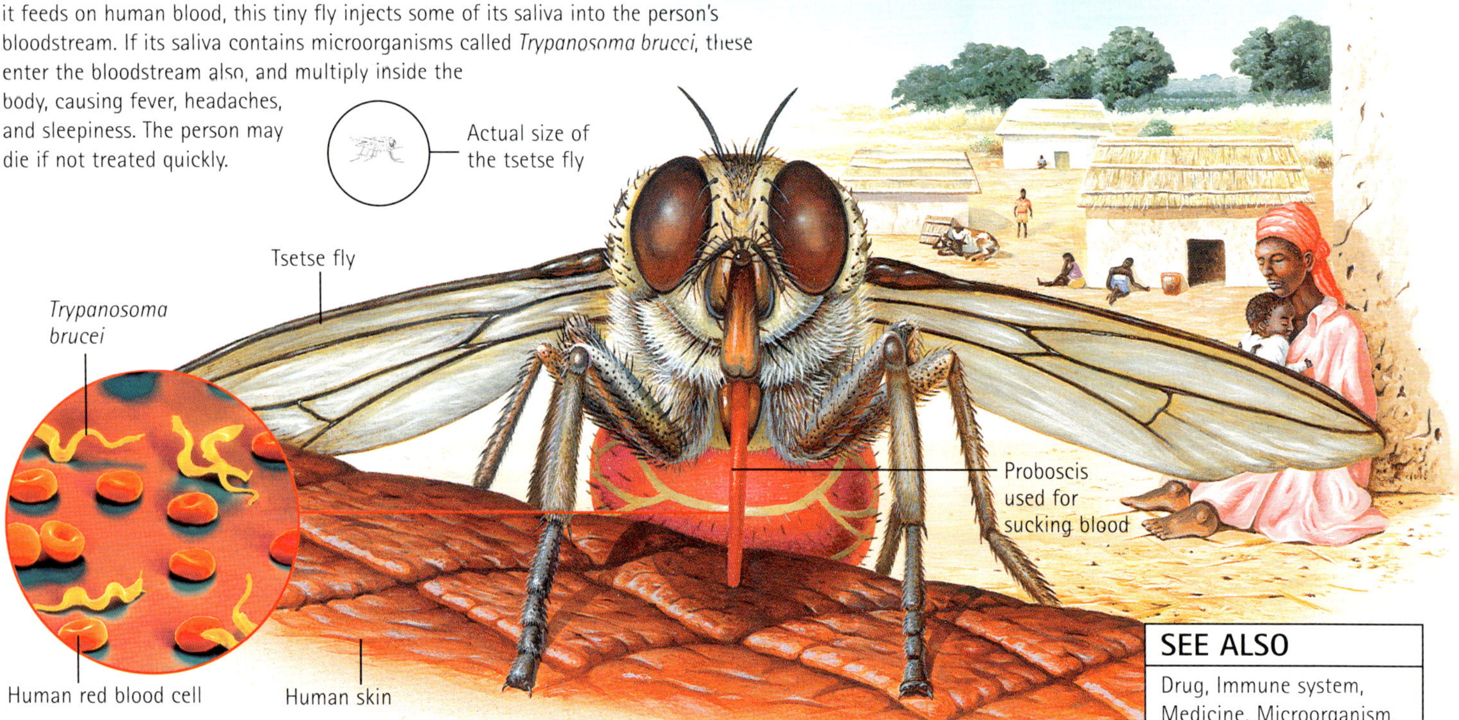

SEE ALSO

Drug, Immune system, Medicine, Microorganism, Surgery

Dog

The domestic dog (*Canis familiaris*) belongs to the dog family, known as Canidae, and is believed to be descended from the gray wolf.

The chihuahua is the world's smallest dog: 10 in. (15cm) to the shoulder.

The poodle is an intelligent dog. There are three types: toy, miniature, and standard.

The greyhound, bred for speed, can reach 35 mph (57kph).

The bulldog was originally bred for the "sport" of bull-baiting in the Middle Ages.

The husky is a powerful sledge dog, able to pull twice its own weight.

The Airedale is the largest breed of terrier, probably bred for hunting otters.

SPORTING DOGS

Sporting dogs are bred for their acute sense of smell, which they use to track down game birds. The pointer (below) was popular during the 1800s, and gets its name from the way it stands with its tail straight and its nose pointing at the hiding bird. Other sporting dogs include setters, which crouch down, or "set," near hiding birds, and retrievers, which fetch dead game.

Dogs were the first animals to be tamed. Fossil remains of a domestic dog dating back 10,500 years have been found in Idaho. The relationship between human and dog probably began because dogs are natural scavengers, and hung around camps looking for food scraps.

BREEDS AND GROUPS

Since then, humans have selectively bred dogs—the American Kennel Club (AKC) recognizes 138 breeds of dog, and Great Britain's Kennel Club includes about 170. These breeds are divided into seven groups by appearance, use, and size: sporting dogs, herding dogs, hounds, nonsporting dogs, terriers, toy dogs, and working dogs.
The dog's most acute senses—smell and hearing—were selectively bred early on for guarding and hunting. Other physical features were bred for specific uses. For example, the dachshund's short legs were selected for going down badger sets, and the bulldog's set-back nose was selected to help it breathe while biting. Nowadays, a gentle, nonaggressive nature is selected for pets.

A DOG'S LIFE

Most domestic dogs are fully grown by the age of 2, are old by the age of 12, and rarely live past 20. Female dogs can become pregnant from about seven months, and give birth to an average of three to six puppies, although some breeds may have up to ten puppies. The puppies open their eyes on the tenth day and are ready to leave their mother at six weeks. Dogs are pack animals and follow a leader. This loyalty can be transferred to a human, especially if the dog is trained while young.

▲ The border collie uses the hunting instincts of its wild ancestors to round up sheep.

SEE ALSO

Hearing, Wolf

DRUG

Drugs are substances that affect the way in which the body or mind works. Most drugs are used medicinally, to cure or prevent an illness.

Over 4,000 years ago, Emperor Chi'en Nung of China put together a book of more than 300 medicinal plants, many of which are still used in medicine today. But it was not until the 1700s, when the English doctor William Withering studied the heart drug digitalis (extracted from foxgloves), that drugs were looked at scientifically. The modern drug industry began in 1899, when the German company Bayer manufactured the painkiller aspirin.

WHICH TYPE OF DRUG?

Doctors use many types of drugs to treat patients. For example, antibiotics such as penicillin kill the bacteria that cause infections. Analgesics (painkillers), such as aspirin and codeine, stop pain messages from reaching the brain. Sedatives have a calming effect and can help a person to sleep. Anesthetics deaden the body's nerves and are used in operations. Vaccines help the immune system to fight diseases, and insulin is given to people when their body fails to make enough of it naturally.

► The foxglove is listed in the oldest surviving book on drugs and their uses, written between A.D. 20 and A.D. 70 by the Ancient Greek doctor Dioscorides.

DANGERS AND ADDICTION

Some drugs, such as heroin or cocaine, are addictive, which means people cannot stop taking them. They are illegal because they are so dangerous. Even medicinal drugs or everyday drugs, such as alcohol, caffeine in tea and coffee, or nicotine in cigarettes, can be harmful if taken in large amounts.

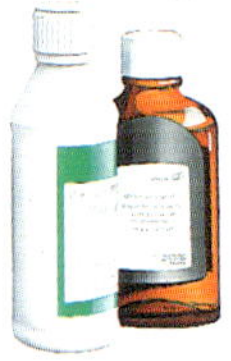

Medicinal liquids called syrups make swallowing drugs easy for children.

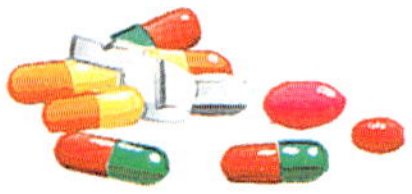

Pills or capsules are the most common form of drug.

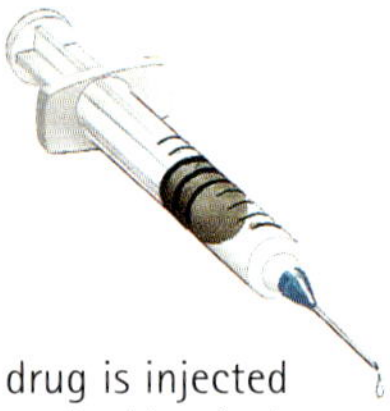

A drug is injected into the blood when a quick response is needed.

Eyedrops and inhalers act fast by sending the drug to the exact spot.

Creams and gels often contain drugs which disinfect a cut or graze.

Skin patches release drugs slowly through the skin into the blood.

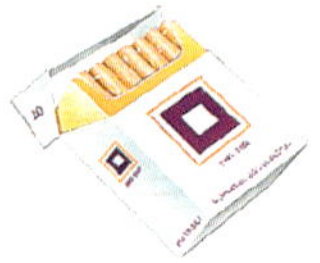

Cigarettes are made from tobacco leaves, which contain the drug nicotine.

TIMED-RELEASE CAPSULES

Drugs sometimes need to be released into the bloodstream slowly over a few hours, especially if they are painkillers. Timed-release capsules contain hundreds of tiny pellets with coatings of different thicknesses. Some of the pellets release the drug in the stomach, others release it later in the intestines.

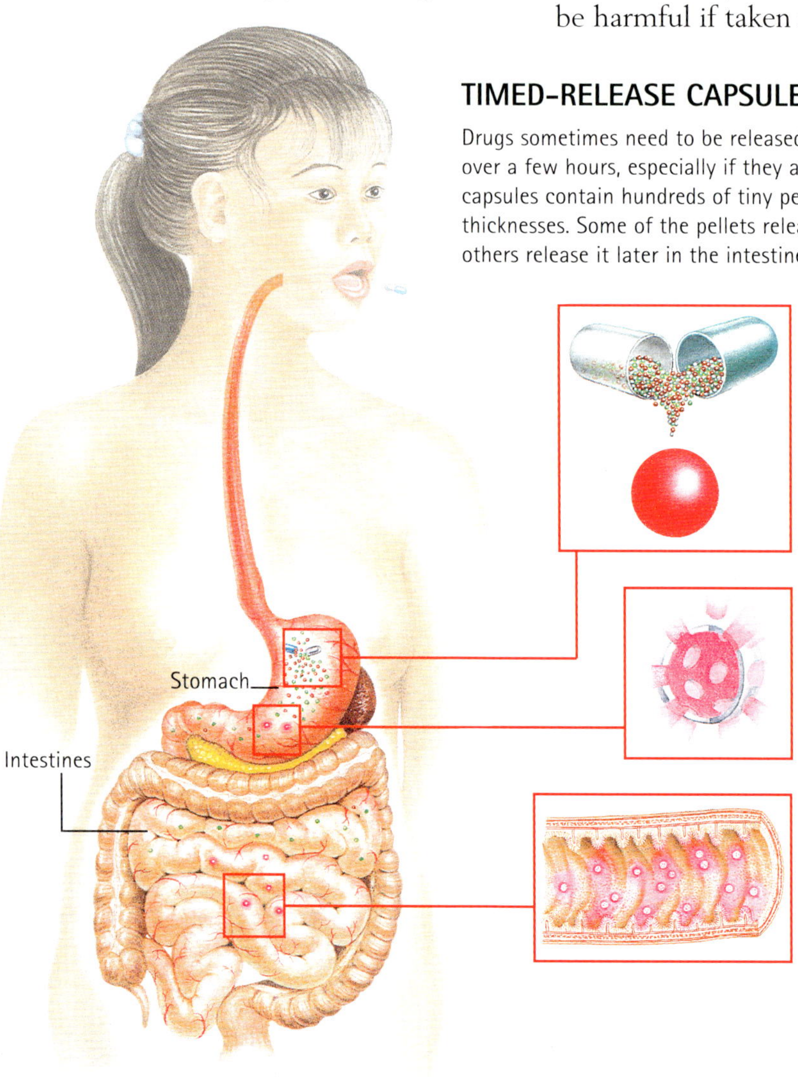

1 The capsule (outer shell) breaks open in the stomach, releasing pellets which contain the drug. Each pellet looks like a tiny ball and is a different color according to the thickness of its coating.

2 The pellets with the thinnest coating dissolve first and release the drug in the stomach. The others move on to the intestines and release the drug later.

3 The drug is absorbed through the walls of the stomach and intestines into the bloodstream.

SEE ALSO
Medicine, Plant

EAGLE AND OTHER BIRDS OF PREY

Eagles and other birds of prey survive by hunting animals. They swoop down on their prey from the air, grabbing them with their sharp talons.

► Unlike hawks and eagles, owls, like this little owl, hunt their prey at night.

The Andean condor is the largest bird of prey. It can weigh 26.5 lb (12kg).

A diving peregrine falcon can reach speeds of over 155 mph (250kph).

Northern goshawks can strike in midair, often attacking from below.

Vultures, such as this black vulture, feed on the bodies of dead animals.

Golden eagles carry prey equal to their own weight in their powerful talons.

Birds of prey are born hunters. They have sharp eyesight to spot far-off prey, sharp, curved talons to catch their food, and strong, hooked beaks to tear at flesh. Most have large, broad wings with flight feathers that spread out when they soar in updrafts. As well as eagles, birds of prey include buzzards, falcons, hawks, kites, ospreys, and vultures. Owls are also often included, but belong to a different bird group.

HUNTING SKILLS

Most birds of prey soar high into the air and then swoop down on their prey on the ground at high speed. Some, such as the peregrine falcon, can also attack birds in midair. The kestrel is unusual because it hovers just a few yards above the ground before swooping. Vultures usually scavenge dead meat.

DIFFERENT TASTES

There are more than 50 species of eagle scattered throughout the world, although many are endangered. Most live in wild, remote places where humans cannot disturb them. Eagles eat a wide range of animals. The golden eagle attacks hares, small rodents, and other birds; the serpent eagle gorges on snakes. Some are experts at snaring fish, and the harpy eagle catches monkeys.

NEST RECYCLING

Many eagles use the same nest, or aerie, again and again, adding more material each time they breed. Their nests can become enormous—a bald eagle's can measure 10 ft. (3m) across and weigh over a ton. Most eagles lay just two eggs. Once the young have hatched, they do not leave the nest for up to two months.

FISH FOR DINNER

The bald eagle, the national bird of the United States, is one of the most endangered birds of prey. It feeds on birds and small animals, but particularly likes fish. It scoops them from the surface of the water and flies off, gripping them in its powerful, sharp talons.

SEE ALSO
Bird

EARTH

Our planet, Earth, is one of the nine planets that move around the Sun. It is made up of rock and metal, and is the only planet known to support life.

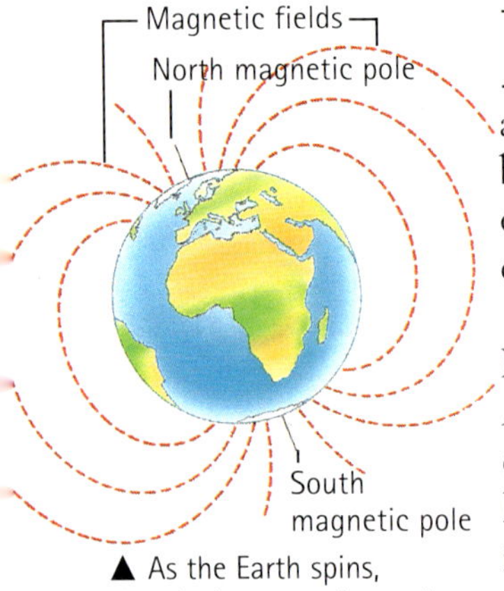

▲ As the Earth spins, electrical currents beneath the surface turn the planet into a huge magnet, with a north and south pole just like any ordinary magnet.

Planet Earth is a not quite perfect ball of rock, with a metal core, which travels around the Sun. It is surrounded by a blanket of gases called the atmosphere, has one moon, and, as far as we know, is the only planet that supports life.

NIGHT AND DAY

Approximately every 24 hours, the Earth does a full circle on its axis—an imaginary line joining the North and South Poles. As it spins, one side turns to face the Sun and is in daylight, while the other side turns away, experiencing night. The Earth spins eastward, which is why the Sun seems to rise in the east and set in the west.

AROUND THE SUN

As well as spinning on its own axis, the Earth is constantly moving around the Sun. One complete path around the Sun is an orbit. The length of a year is determined by the time it takes a planet to make one orbit. This means that Earth travels 595 million miles (958 million km), at an average speed of 19 mi./sec. (30km/sec).

CHANGING SEASONS

The Earth is tilted toward the Sun at an angle of 23.5°. As the Earth orbits, those places that are tilted toward the Sun receive more warmth and light for the part of the year that is known as summer. As these places move farther around, they tilt away from the Sun, experiencing winter.

CORE TO CRUST

Beneath its thin shell, or crust, the interior of the Earth is very hot. Below about 45 mi. (70km), there is a mantle of rock that is semimolten (partly melted). The outer layer of the Earth's core is molten too, but enormous pressure keeps the inner core (the center) solid, even though temperatures here reach over 10,800°F (6,000°C). The upper layer of the mantle is made of plates, like pieces of a jigsaw, with the continents on top. Sometimes, the plates rub together, causing pressure which escapes through volcanoes or earthquakes.

FROM CORE TO CRUST

If we could cut a large section out of the Earth, we would see a planet made in four layers. At its center is a solid inner core of almost pure iron, surrounded by an outer core of liquid iron and nickel. Enveloping this is a mantle of silicon compounds, crystals, and lighter metals topped with a hard rock crust.

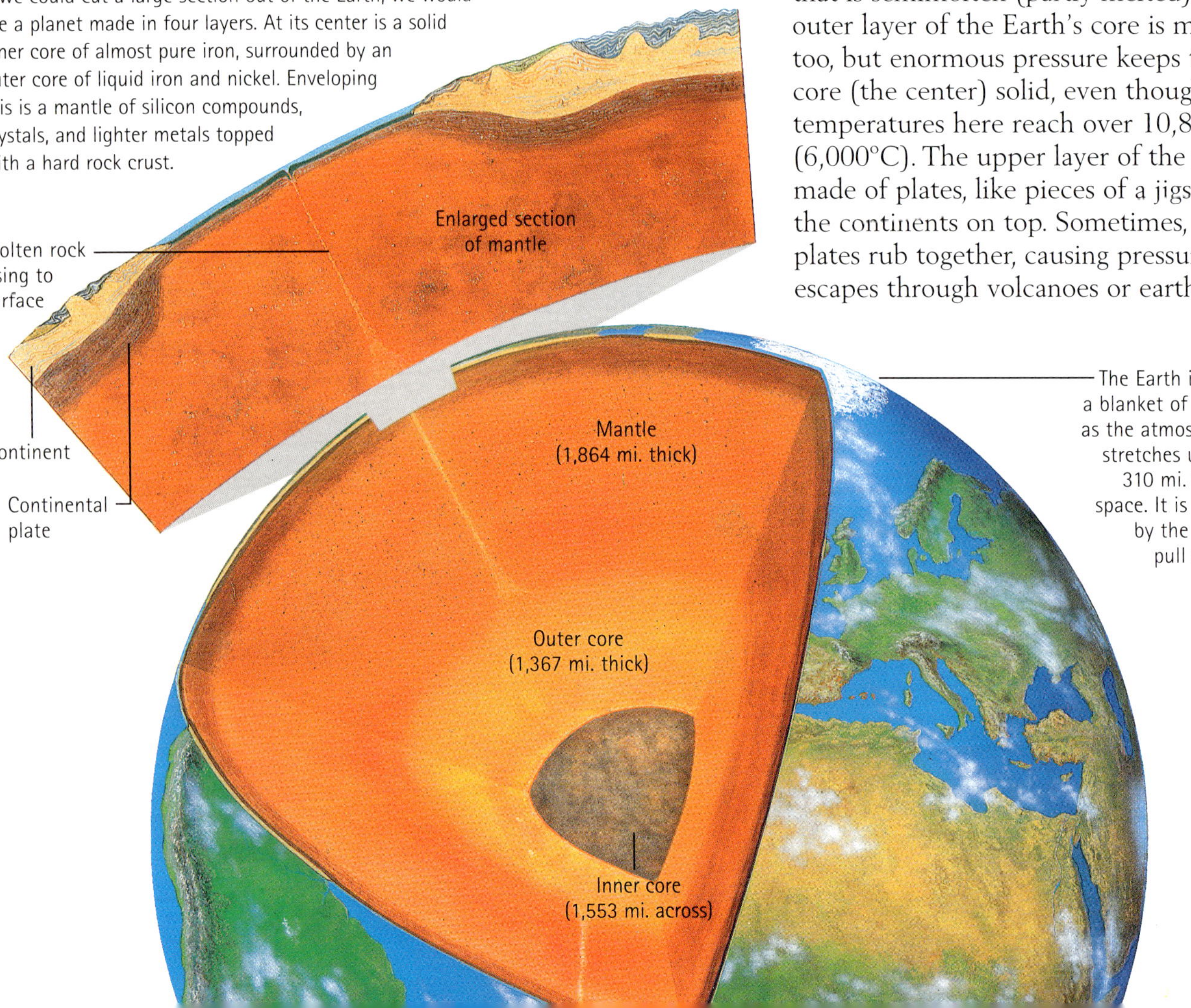

The Earth is wrapped in a blanket of gases known as the atmosphere, which stretches up more than 310 mi. (500km) into space. It is held in place by the gravitational pull of the planet

THE EVOLVING EARTH

Astronomers believe that the Earth began to form about 4.6 billion years ago, when the solar nebula (a vast cloud of hot debris circling the newly formed Sun) began to cluster together into lumps that eventually became the planets of our solar system. The process took millions of years to complete, and Earth, like the other planets, developed a unique chemistry and atmosphere.

1 Hot clouds of dust and gases spin around the newly formed Sun. As the specks of dust collide, they stick together in lumps.

2 The forces of gravity pull more passing lumps into the spinning ball. Heavy elements such as iron sink to the center.

3 Lighter metals and rocks come to the surface and the red-hot Earth cools enough for a hard shell to form.

4 Gases escaping from the Earth form clouds and rain falls, creating oceans containing small oxygen-producing plants.

5 Originally one large mass, the Earth's land surface is now split into seven large bodies, known as continents.

LIFE ON EARTH

Why exactly there is life on Earth is still a mystery to scientists. The theories are numerous, but the answer is probably a combination of reasons. First, Earth's distance from the Sun is ideal—not too hot like Venus, nor too cold like Mars. Second, Earth is the only planet we know of that has water on its surface—over 70 percent of it is covered by water. Scientists believe that electrical storms on the newly formed planet caused chemical reactions between gases in the atmosphere. These created the first building blocks of life, which fell into the oceans, where they combined to become simple plant-like forms. All plants make oxygen, and so an ideal atmosphere was soon created for the evolution of oxygen-breathing life-forms.

▲ A day is the time it takes the Earth to turn once on its own axis: 23 hr., 56 min., and 4 sec.

▲ A lunar month is the time it takes the Moon to travel once around the Earth: 28 days.

▲ A year is the time it takes the Earth to travel once around the Sun: 365 days, 6 hr., and 9 min.

EARTH FACTS AND FIGURES

- Earth's diameter (the distance from Pole to Pole through the center) is 7,900 mi. (12,714km)
- Earth's circumference (the distance around its middle at the equator) is 24,901 mi. (40,075km)
- As Earth spins, places near the equator move much faster than places at the Poles, causing the planet to bulge slightly in the middle and be flattened at the top and bottom
- The temperature of Earth's inner core may be as hot as 11,200°F (6,200°C)
- Of the nine planets in our solar system, Earth is the third closest to the Sun
- The Sun and the Earth are about 93 million miles (150 million km) apart
- Earth's path around the Sun is not a circle but an ellipse (an oval), which means it is closer to the Sun on January 1 than on June 1

SEE ALSO

Atmosphere, Big Bang theory, Continent, Earthquake, Evolution, Gravity, Magnetism, Planet, Season, Solar system, Sun, Time, Volcano

EARTHQUAKE

An earthquake is a shaking of the Earth's surface. It is caused by the sudden release of pressure through weak parts of the Earth's crust.

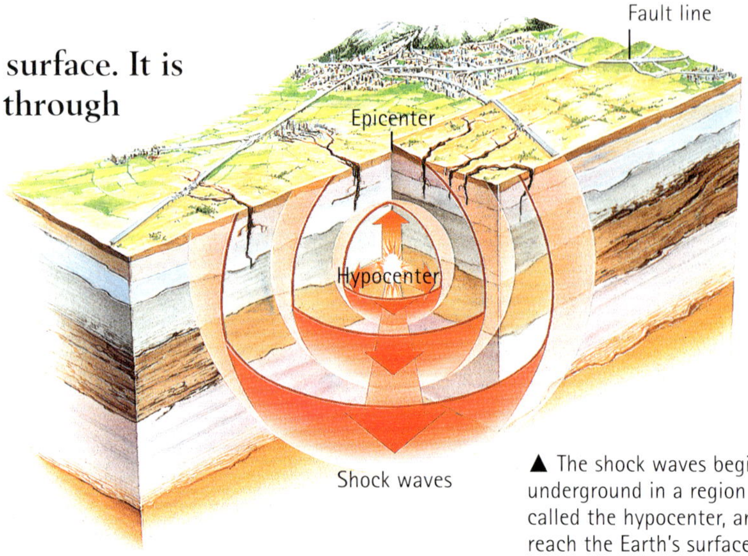

▲ The shock waves begin underground in a region called the hypocenter, and reach the Earth's surface directly above, at the epicenter. From here, they radiate in all directions.

The vast majority of earthquakes do not cause any serious damage. Small tremors can happen with an erupting volcano, an avalanche, or a landslide. However, the largest earthquakes occur as a result of pressure or tension deep under the ground being released through weak areas (fault lines) in the Earth's crust.

TECTONIC PLATES

The Earth's crust is broken into giant slabs called tectonic plates. Sometimes, pressure builds up underground as a result of the plates moving against each other. The pressure is suddenly released, sending out shock waves in all directions and causing the Earth's crust to shake and even crack.

EARTHQUAKE ZONES

There are two great earthquake zones. Both are where two tectonic plates meet. One stretches across southern Asia, through the Mediterranean, and into eastern Africa. The other is the "ring of fire" around the Pacific Ocean, which includes the United States. In 1906, a large part of San Francisco was destroyed by an earthquake in this zone.

SHOCK WAVES

Earthquake shock waves are known as seismic waves. They are detected using a measuring instrument called a seismometer. A severe earthquake can be felt as much as 250 mi. (400km) away. The intensity of an earthquake is plotted on the Richter scale. An earthquake measuring over 7 on this scale can destroy buildings and take lives.

DISASTER IN JAPAN

In 1995, the Japanese city of Kobe was devastated by a violent earthquake that killed over 5,000 people. The earthquake measured 7.2 on the Richter scale. It caused houses and apartments to collapse, trains to be derailed, and roads to be ripped apart. The shaking lasted for about 20 seconds.

SEE ALSO

Continent, Earth, Mountain and valley, Ocean and sea

Eastern Europe

Eastern Europe is a geographical region of eight countries that were once part of the communist bloc controlled by the Soviet Union.

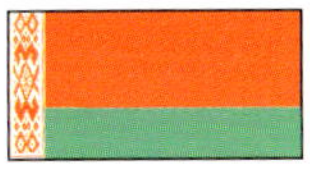

BELARUS
Area: 88,044 sq. mi.
Population: 10,339,000
Capital: Minsk
Languages: Belarussian and Russian
Currency: Rouble

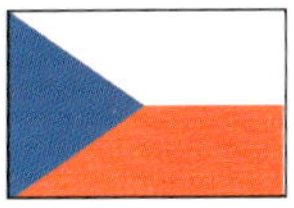

CZECH REPUBLIC
Area: 30,448 sq. mi.
Population: 10,332,000
Capital: Prague
Language: Czech
Currency: Koruna

HUNGARY
Area: 35,912 sq. mi.
Population: 10,229,000
Capital: Budapest
Language: Hungarian
Currency: Forint

MOLDOVA
Area: 13,100 sq. mi.
Population: 4,344,000
Capital: Chisinau
Language: Moldovan
Currency: Leu

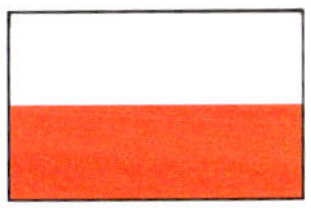

POLAND
Area: 120,355 sq. mi.
Population: 38,612,000
Capital: Warsaw
Language: Polish
Currency: Zloty

Eastern Europe lies between the Baltic Sea, the Balkan Peninsula, the Black Sea, and Russia. It makes up more than one sixth of Europe's land area, and is a region of plains, low hills, and mountains.

PEAKS AND PLAINS

To the south lie the rugged Carpathian Mountains and Transylvanian Alps. The highest point is Gerlachovsky Stit, a peak of 8,713 ft. (2,656m) in the Carpathians. To the west is the Hungarian Plain, and to the east are the vast rolling steppes (treeless plains) of the Ukraine.

A REGION OF RIVERS

The area is watered by some of Europe's major rivers. The Danube, Europe's second longest river at 1,725 mi. (2,776km), forms much of Romania's southwestern border; the Dnieper and the Dniester both flow through the Ukraine. Europe's largest swamp, the Pripet Marshes, straddles the border between Belarus and the Ukraine.

▲ Expanses of steppe once covered the Ukraine, but this land, covered with rich soil, is now heavily farmed.

CONTINENTAL CLIMATE

Away from the mountains, Eastern Europe has warm summers; temperatures average 68°F (20°C) or more in July. Winters get colder as you travel from west to east. Most of the region has moderate rainfall, with 20–40 in. (500–1,000mm) per year, but the southeast is drier, with less than 20 in. (500mm) of rain per year.

BREADBASKET OF EUROPE

In the lowlands, many of the region's forests have been cleared for farming. The fertile steppes, once an area of natural grassland, are also farmed. The Ukraine is sometimes called "the breadbasket of Europe" because of its high production of grain and other crops. ▶

▼ The medieval city of Prague, capital of the Czech Republic, has some of Europe's most beautiful and well-preserved architecture.

ROMANIA
Area: 91,934 sq. mi.
Population: 22,692,000
Capital: Bucharest
Language: Romanian
Currency: Leu

SLOVAKIA
Area: 18,925 sq. mi.
Population: 5,369,000
Capital: Bratislava
Language: Slovak
Currency: Koruna

UKRAINE
Area: 222,600 sq. mi.
Population: 51,550,000
Capital: Kiev
Language: Ukrainian
Currency: Hryvna

DISAPPEARING WILDLIFE

As in the rest of Europe, the wildlife in Eastern Europe has been reduced by the destruction of forests and grasslands. A number of large mammals that once grazed on the steppes, such as the saiga antelope, have now disappeared. The rare wisent (European bison) is found in western Belarus and central Poland; the Danube Delta on the Black Sea is a major wetland and home to many birds.

HEAVY AND LIGHT INDUSTRY

Coal, oil and natural gas, iron ore, and other minerals are found in this region. Heavy industry produces machinery,

▶ Old-fashioned factories, such as this one in Romania, cause air, water, and soil pollution in many parts of Eastern Europe.

▲ The practice of Eastern Orthodox Christianity is widespread in Belarus, Moldova, Romania, and the Ukraine. Here, priests celebrate the Eucharist in Kiev in the Ukraine.

transportation equipment, and steel and the manufacture of electronic goods, clothes, and processed food is increasing.

CITY DWELLERS

Many people live in rural areas, and a few people still follow nomadic lifestyles. But about two thirds of the people live and work in towns and cities. Kiev, in the Ukraine, is the largest city in Eastern Europe, with a population of 2,651,000.

RELIGIOUS WORSHIP

Religion is an important part of life for many people in Eastern Europe. The two dominant faiths in the region are Roman Catholic and Eastern Orthodox Christianity. There is a Muslim minority in Romania, which was once part of the Muslim Ottoman Empire.

FOREIGN POWERS

All of the countries of Eastern Europe have at times in their history been under the influence of a foreign power. In 1793, Poland disappeared after being divided up among Prussia, Austria, and Russia. Hungary and Czechoslovakia formed part of the Habsburg Empire until 1918. Romania gained its independence from Turkey in 1878. More recently, the Ukraine, Belarus, and Moldova were part of the Russian-dominated Soviet Union.

COMMUNIST RULE

After World War II, all the countries of Eastern Europe came under communist rule, either as part of the Soviet Union or as members of the Soviet bloc. Romania remained outside Soviet control, but under the communist dictator Nicolae Ceauşescu.

THE NEW MAP

In the late 1980s, the countries of Eastern Europe began to abandon communist rule in favor of their own democratically elected governments. Belarus, Moldova, and the Ukraine gained their independence in 1991, following the breakup of the Soviet Union. In 1993, Czechoslovakia split peacefully into two countries: the Czech Republic and Slovakia.

▲ Vacationers in Budapest play chess in one of Hungary's many natural hot springs.

DEMOCRACY IN HUNGARY

From the end of World War II, Hungary, like the rest of Eastern Europe, came under Soviet communist rule. However, demonstrations in favor of democracy, such as this one in Budapest in 1988, indicated people's unhappiness with the government. In 1989, Hungary was the first Eastern European country to shake off communism. In March 1990, it elected its first democratic government in 42 years.

SEE ALSO

Cold War, Communism, Democracy, Europe, Russia and the Baltic States

ECOLOGY

Ecology is the study of how plants, animals, and humans live together in their natural surroundings, and the ways in which they affect one another.

THE FOOD CHAIN

Each organism in a food chain feeds on and gets energy from the previous level. Ecologists divide plants and animals in a chain into groups, depending on how they get their energy. Plants are energy producers, using the sun's energy to produce new growth. Animals are consumers, obtaining energy by eating plants or other animals.

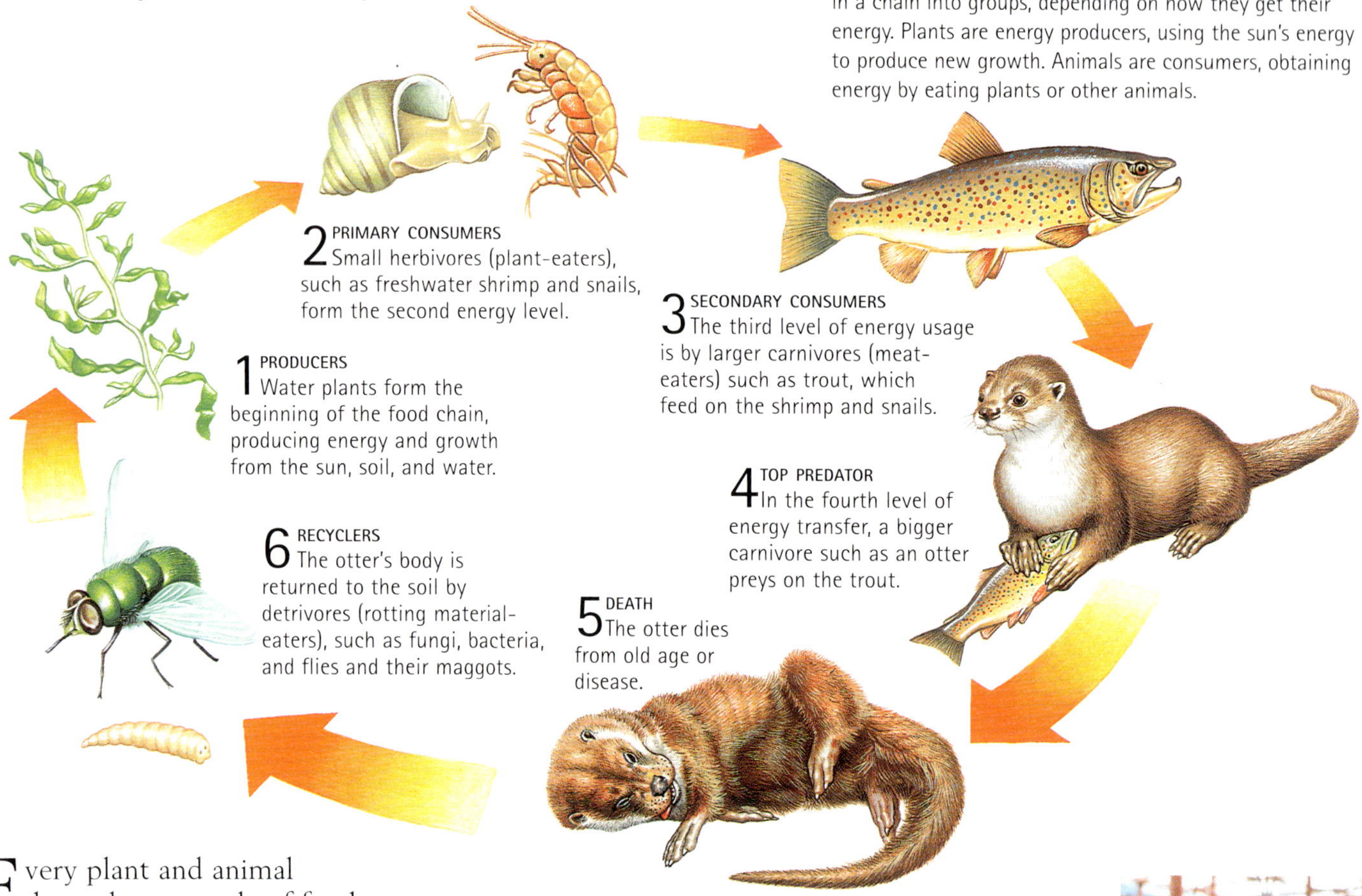

Every plant and animal depends on a cycle of food, energy, and waste disposal that links it to other plants and animals. Ecologists study how plants and animals are linked to each other in food chains and webs.

CHAINED TOGETHER

All living things need energy. Plants use light energy from the sun to turn substances in the soil, air, and water into food. Insects eat the plants and fish, birds, and other animals eat the insects. In this way, energy is passed along a food chain. When living things die, their bodies break down and release nutrients back into the ground to start the process again.

ECOSYSTEMS

An ecosystem consists of the plants and animals in a certain area, together with the air, soil, climate, and other nonliving things. A forest is one type of ecosystem, but there are many others. An ecosystem can be as small as a pond or as large as an ocean.

HUMANS INTERVENE

Humans are part of the biggest ecosystem of all—the Earth itself. Some human actions can affect the entire planet. Logging a rain forest, for example, affects the forest by destroying its plants and animals. Since trees produce the oxygen needed by humans and other life-forms, the world's oxygen supply is also affected.

GRAY SQUIRREL INVASION

The introduction of plants or animals from foreign lands can have harmful effects on ecology. When gray squirrels from North America were introduced to Britain, the native red squirrels were pushed out of the food chain in most areas.

▲ Many timber companies manage their forests ecologically, using a process known as artificial reforestation. This means that a constant supply of seed is sown in a nursery and transplanted to the forest to replace felled trees.

SEE ALSO

Animal, Brazil, Conservation, Forest, Habitat, Plant, Pollution

EDUCATION

Education is the development of skills and knowledge. It can be formal, as provided by schools, or informal—through playing, watching, and learning in everyday life.

Learning to play a musical instrument is free as part of the curriculum in some countries. In other places, pupils must pay for lessons.

School trips are a fun and exciting way of relating subjects learned in the classroom to real-life objects and situations.

Many people feel that the main reason for educating children is to benefit society, by teaching skills needed to keep the community going. Others feel that it is more important to develop an individual's talents and interests. The Ancient Greek philosopher Socrates believed that education could make people happier.

SCHOOL FOR ALL

The Ancient Greeks were the first to set up a formal education system, but only for boys of rich families. Lessons included the art of public speaking for budding politicians. In many countries, the church or charities governed schooling. It wasn't until the 1800s that governments began to take control, and the 1900s before education became free for most girls and boys. However, millions of people worldwide still do not possess the basic skills of reading and writing.

BEST YEARS OF YOUR LIFE

In most countries, it is compulsory for children to go to primary school at the age of 5 or 6, then on to a secondary (high) school at about 13 years of age. Some start earlier. Friedrich Froebel opened the first kindergarten (nursery) in Germany in 1837. In many parts of the world, attendance drops after the age of 11, but education can continue into adulthood at colleges or universities. Courses offer vocational (career) training or specialist qualifications.

THE CURRICULUM

The curriculum (subjects taught) varies in each country. It may emphasize religion, local crafts, or history. Many schools in the 1800s concentrated on reading, writing, and arithmetic. Subjects and teaching methods have changed over the years, as have educational theories. The Czech educationalist Comenius (1592–1670) thought pictures were a vital teaching tool. Italian reformer Maria Montessori (1870–1952) created wooden devices to help children learn through exploration.

SCHOOLS OF THOUGHT

Styles of teaching, subjects taught, and classroom settings have changed over the years. Once children had to sit in rows in silence while the teacher lectured them. Now, there is more emphasis on interaction and small-group tuition. Educators argue about which is best—formal instruction (presenting facts to learn) or learning through activity and experience.

▲ A government health advisor known as the Food Fairy visits a classroom in the United States in 1925 to instruct children on healthy eating.

SEE ALSO
Greece (Ancient)

EGYPT

Egypt lies in the northeast of Africa. It has more people than any other African nation except Nigeria, yet most Egyptians live in just four percent of the country.

Area: 386,198 sq. mi.
Population: 57,800,000
Capital: Cairo
Language: Arabic
Currency: Egyptian pound

Most of Egypt's people live around the Nile Delta and Valley and along the Suez Canal, a vital shipping link for world trade. The Nile River, controlled by the Aswan High Dam, provides fertile land stretching from Egypt's border with Sudan right up to the Mediterranean Sea. Egypt's main cities are its capital, Cairo, and the port of Alexandria—two of the largest cities in Africa.

Traders, such as this man selling herbs and tea, set up their stalls in open street markets, or bazaars.

DESERT AREAS

On either side of the Nile lie two deserts that together cover more than 90 percent of the country—the vast, low-lying Western Desert and the hilly Eastern Desert, which borders the Red Sea.

AGRICULTURAL LIFE

Agriculture is the country's most important industry, employing over a third of all Egyptians. These farmers, known as *fellahin*, grow cotton and food crops such as corn and rice in the fertile Nile Delta. The manufacturing industry is growing, and tourists attracted by the ancient ruins also generate income for many Egyptians. Cotton, oil, and cloth are major exports.

A MUSLIM POPULATION

Most Egyptians are descended from the people of Ancient Egypt or from Arabs who invaded the country in the A.D. 600s. About 90 percent of the people are Muslim.

EGYPT TODAY

Egypt was part of the Ottoman Empire from 1517 until 1922. Britain controlled the Suez Canal and had administrative power in the country from the 1880s until the 1950s. Since the 1980s, Egypt has strengthened its ties with other Arab nations, including Saudi Arabia.

Egypt's main port of Alexandria was the world's greatest trading city 2,000 years ago.

▶ Triangular-sailed wooden boats called *feluccas* carry goods and passengers along the Nile.

SEE ALSO
Africa, Egypt (Ancient), Islam, Middle East

Egypt, Ancient

Ancient Egypt developed along the Nile River around 5,000 years ago. Over the next 2,500 years, it grew into one of the greatest civilizations of all time.

The funeral mask of Tutankhamen, boy-king of Egypt (1361-52 B.C.), was discovered in 1922.

The tombs of some important officials contained models of items that they might need in the next world.

The Ancient Egyptians chose to settle by the Nile in Africa because each year the river flooded, spreading mud over the banks. This provided them with fertile land to farm.

PYRAMID BUILDERS

The Ancient Egyptians were the first real engineers and built impressive temples, cities, and pyramids. The largest of the pyramids needed over 2 million blocks, each weighing as much as 2.5 tons. Some of the stones were from distant quarries and carried down the Nile on rafts.

A CREATIVE PEOPLE

The Ancient Egyptians used papyrus reeds to make shoes, boats, ropes, and writing paper. Papyrus scrolls preserve Ancient Egyptian hieroglyphic writing. The Egyptians also invented a 365-day calendar.

▲ Pyramids were burial monuments for kings. The Sphinx (half man, half lion) stands beside the pyramids at Giza.

LIFE AFTER DEATH

Many gods were worshiped, including the sun god Ra and Osiris, god of the dead. The Egyptian kings, or pharaohs, were also believed to be gods. When they died, the kings and queens were buried in tombs full of things needed in the next world—food, jewelry, even small statues of servants (*shabtis*). Most royal tombs were robbed, but in 1922, the tomb of the boy pharaoh Tutankhamen was found, with most of its treasures untouched.

END OF A CIVILIZATION

Ancient Egypt included three great ages: the Old Kingdom, the Middle Kingdom, and the New Kingdom. In 31 B.C. Cleopatra died, and Egypt fell to the Roman Empire.

MUMMIFIED BODIES

The Ancient Egyptians believed in life after death. Their bodies were mummified (preserved) before burial to prevent decay. It took 70 days to mummify a body.

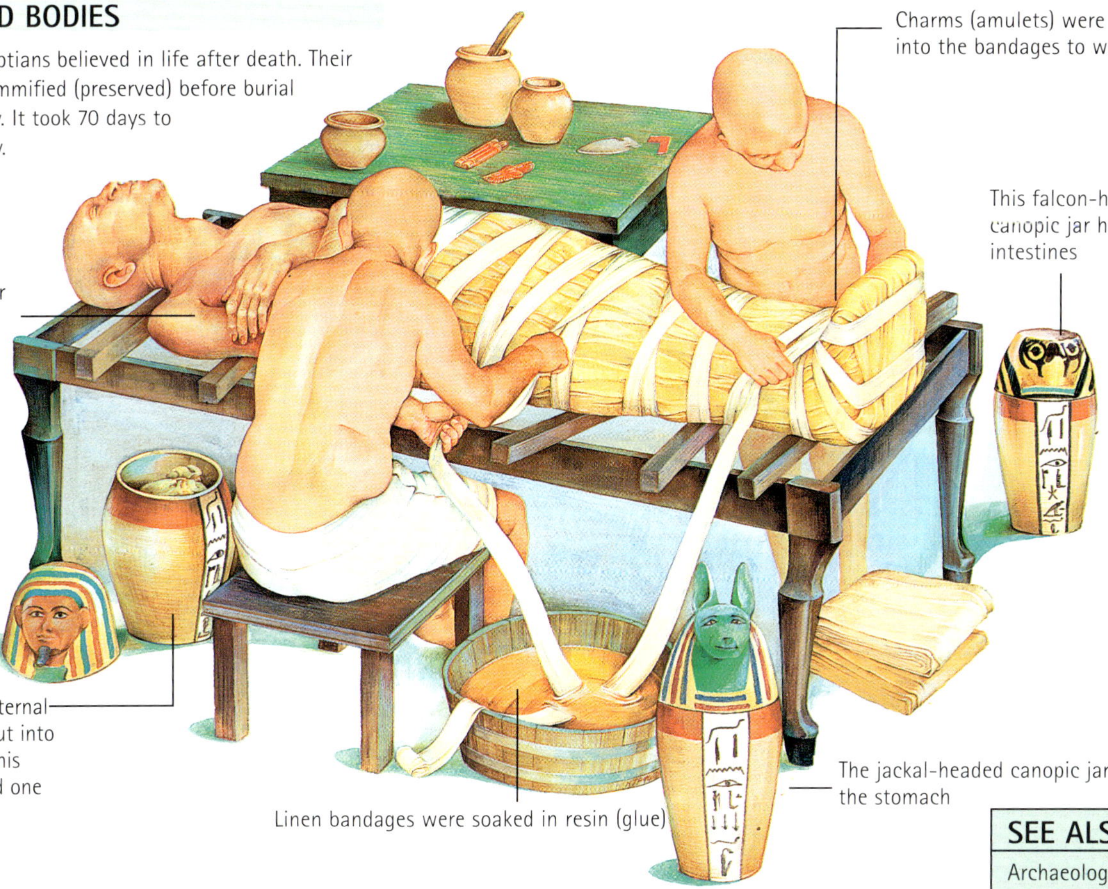

Charms (amulets) were wrapped into the bandages to ward off evil

This falcon-headed canopic jar held the intestines

The body was placed in salt for 40 days to dry. Before being bandaged, the dried body was rubbed with oils and spices

Most of the internal organs were put into canopic jars. This human-headed one held the liver

Linen bandages were soaked in resin (glue)

The jackal-headed canopic jar held the stomach

SEE ALSO

Archaeology, Egypt, Paper, Roman Empire

ELECTRICITY

Electricity is a form of energy. It can be stored in batteries or sent along wires to make electric trains, computers, lightbulbs, and other devices work.

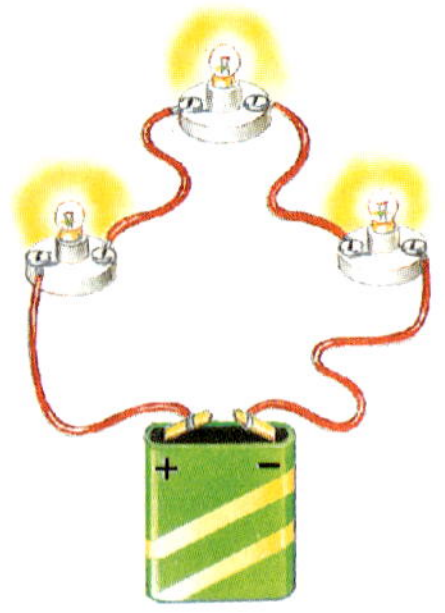

▲ Each lightbulb in a circuit creates resistance to the flow of electric current, and so lightbulbs wired in series do not glow brightly.

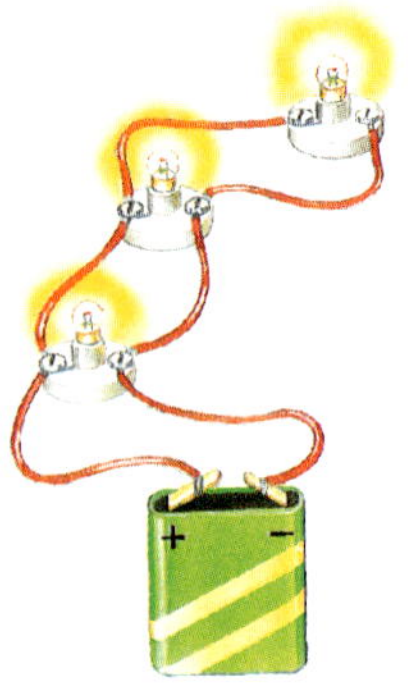

▲ Lightbulbs wired in parallel all glow brightly, because each lightbulb is connected directly to the battery.

Electricity is an invisible form of energy created by the movement of charged particles. It flows into our homes along wires and can be easily converted into other energy forms, such as heat and light.

PASSING ON ELECTRONS

Everything in the world, including humans and the air they breathe, is made of atoms. Each of these tiny particles has a positively charged center (nucleus), with smaller, negatively charged electrons whizzing around it. Electricity is created when one of the electrons jumps to another atom. This can be caused by the magnetic field in a generator, by chemicals in a battery, or by friction (rubbing materials together).

THALES THE PHILOSOPHER

The discovery that an electric charge could be created by rubbing two materials together was first made by the Greek philosopher Thales over 2,600 years ago. He found that if he rubbed the fossilized tree sap, amber, with silk, it attracted feathers and dust. We now know that this happened because electrons had been passed between the silk and the amber,

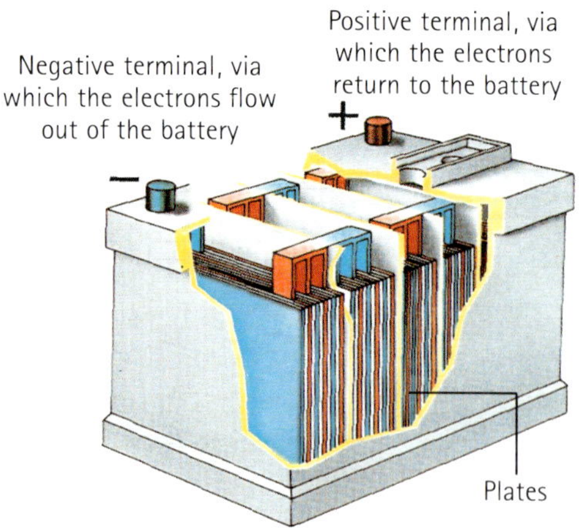

▲ Wet batteries, like those in cars, store electricity and can be recharged. Six cells contain lead and lead dioxide plates in a solution of dilute sulfuric acid. The battery is first charged by an outside electrical source, but after that a generator, run by the car's engine, keeps it charged.

making them electrically charged. In recognition of his discovery, our word electron comes from the Greek word *elecktron*, meaning amber.

CONDUCTORS AND INSULATORS

The electricity of substances like amber is called static electricity, because the charge stays in place once the electrons have moved between the atoms. In other substances, the electrons carry on flowing. These substances are called conductors. Most electrical wires are made of copper because it is a good electrical conductor, as are all metals. Water also conducts electricity, which is why it is dangerous to

HOW A GENERATOR WORKS

An electric generator works by using the principle of electromagnetic induction, discovered in 1831 by the British chemist and physicist Michael Faraday (1791–1867). He discovered that if a coil of wire is spun between two magnets, electrons begin to flow inside the wire coil. An alternating current (AC) and a direct current (DC) can be created in this way.

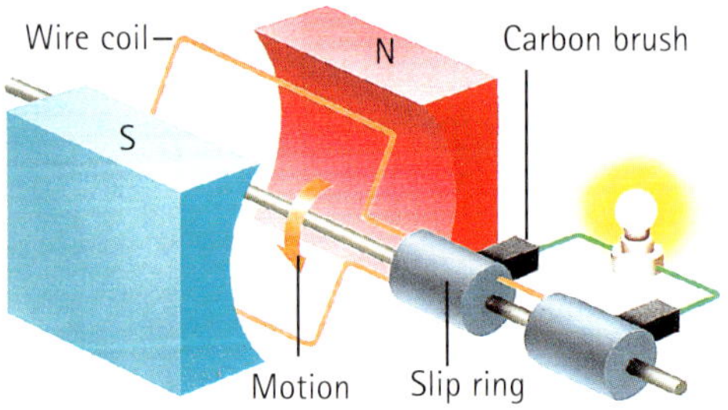

▲ The two magnets naturally produce an alternating current (AC). As the coil spins, the magnetic field inside the coil points first one way and then the other. This makes the electric current change direction, or alternate.

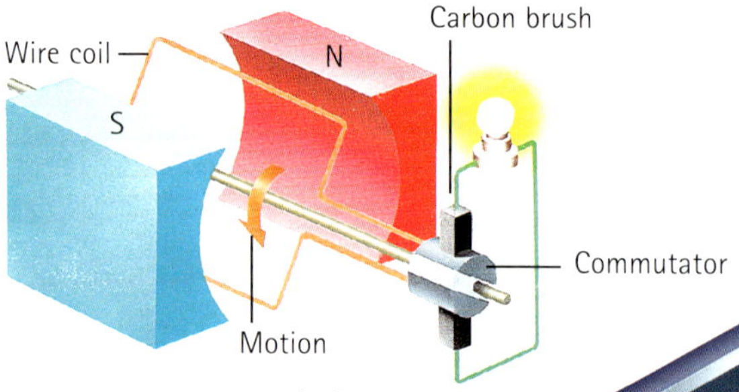

▲ To create a direct current (DC), which flows in only one direction, the coil must be attached to a device called a commutator which is able to reverse the current.

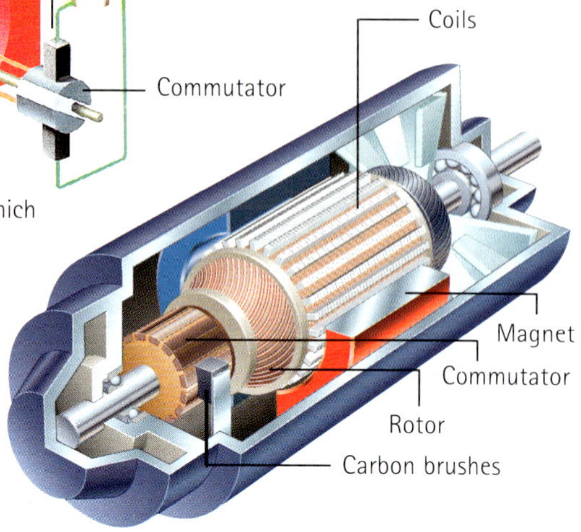

► Practical DC generators are used to power large industrial motors. Unlike Faraday's simple model, a generator has many coils of wire wound on a rotor.

ELECTRICAL TERMS

Conductor Any substance through which an electric current can flow

Coulomb (C) The measurement of electric charge

Current How fast electrons flow along a conductor—it is measured in amperes (A)

Insulator Any substance through which an electric current cannot flow

Resistance How hard it is for current to flow through a conductor—it is measured in ohms (Ω)

Static electricity Electric charge created by two objects rubbing together and exchanging electrons

Voltage (V) A unit of measurement describing how powerfully a battery sends electric current

Watt A unit of measurement that describes how much electrical energy can be converted into heat and light energy per second

operate electrical appliances with wet hands. Other materials are made of atoms between which it is almost impossible for electrons to flow. These materials are known as insulators, and include plastic, wood, and amber. A flow of electrons is known as a current, and the term "resistance" is a measure of how difficult it is for current to flow through a conductor.

COMPLETING THE CIRCUIT

For an electrical appliance such as a flashlight to work, its electricity source (the battery) must be connected to the bulb by wires in an unbroken loop: a circuit. The job of the flashlight's on/off switch is to open or close a gap in the circuit. When the switch is on, electricity flows around the circuit, lighting the bulb. When the switch is off, the circuit is broken and the current cannot flow.

MAIN POWER SUPPLY

Batteries can provide only a limited amount of electricity. So most electrical devices receive their power from a main power supply, or electricity distribution mains. Wires connect millions of wall sockets to a power plant. An electric current flows from the plant, along the wires, out of the sockets, and into the equipment being used. To complete the circuit, the current returns to the power plant through other wires.

PRODUCING ELECTRICITY

All power plants have a generator which produces electricity. In nuclear power plants, the nuclear reactor creates the heat needed to turn water into steam. The steam turns giant wheels, called turbines, which power the generator. The electricity it produces then flows along wires to homes, offices, schools, and stores.

THE POWER PLANT

The nuclear reactor splits atoms to create the heat needed to produce steam to spin the turbines.

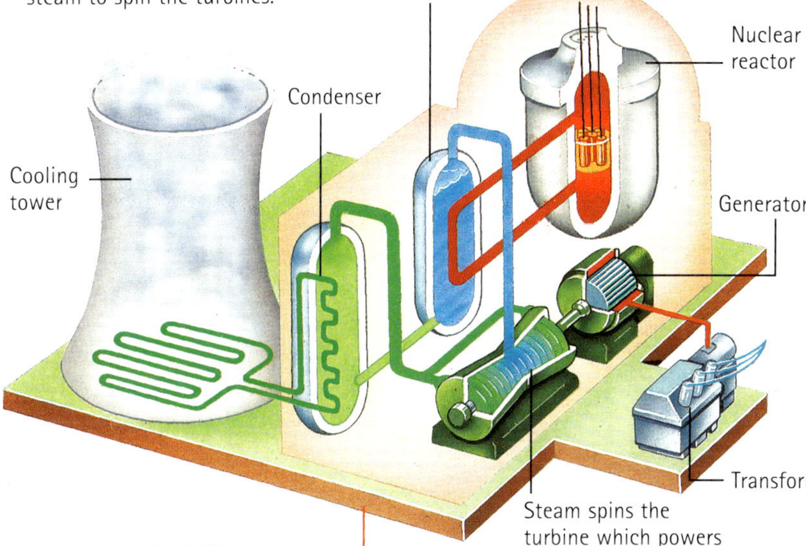

THE ELECTRICITY GRID

Electricity from the power plant travels via step-up and step-down transformers, which convert it to the voltage needed for distribution.

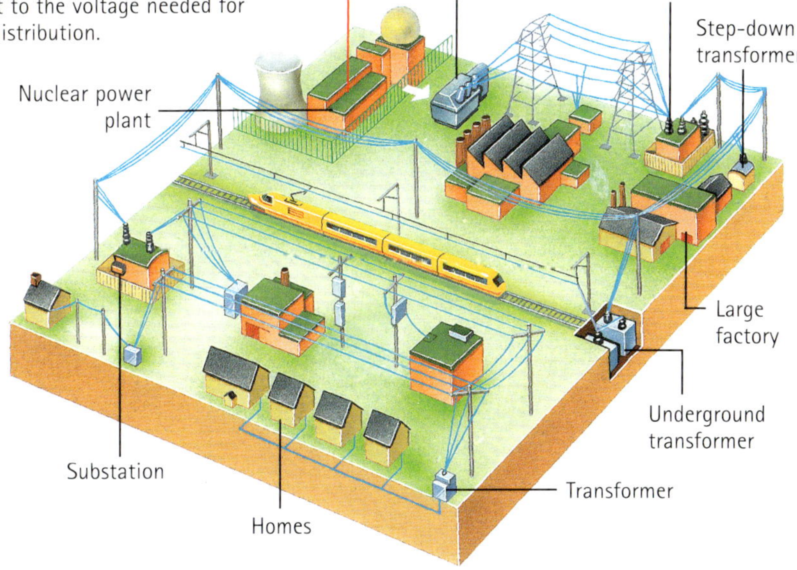

ALTERNATING CURRENT

The electricity that comes out of a power plant is in the form of alternating current (AC). Unlike a battery, which produces a steady one-way current called a direct current (DC), the main power supply flows first in one direction and then the other. The current changes direction very rapidly (about 60 times a second).

SEE ALSO

Atom and molecule, Electronics, Energy, Heat, Magnetism, Nuclear power

Electronics

Electronics is a branch of engineering which studies the components and circuits that make up modern electrical devices, like radios and toasters.

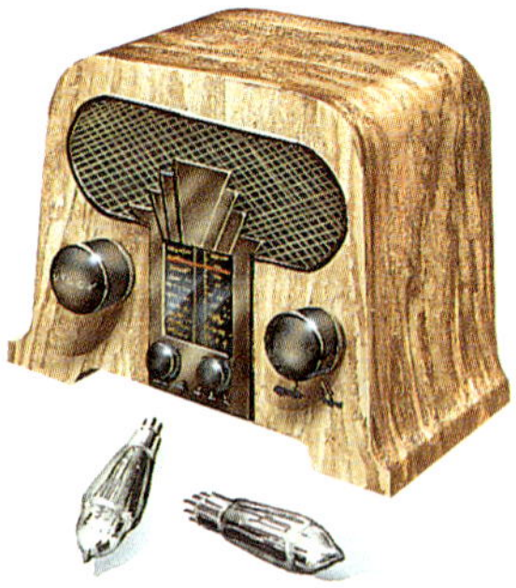

Until the 1950s, radios used glass tubes. They were bulky and fragile.

In the 1950s, the small, durable transistor began to replace the valve.

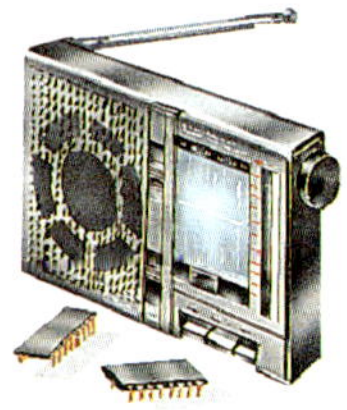

In the 1970s, microchips made hand-size radio-cassette players possible.

Modern electrical devices contain tiny electronic parts called components, which are joined together by lines of metallic paint on circuit boards. Electronic engineers know how to put the right components together to make circuits that can perform specific jobs.

WORKING PARTS

Components affect the way electrons (tiny charged particles) flow through a circuit. The simplest component, the switch, breaks the flow of electrons, or current. Resistors make it harder for the current to flow, while capacitors store current as electrical charge. Diodes let current flow in only one direction.

TRANSISTOR TECHNOLOGY

The first circuits used bulky glass vacuum tubes, which could magnify a current or switch it on or off. This ability to turn a current on or off electronically is the principle behind all computers. In the 1950s, the valve was replaced by a device called the transistor, which was much smaller, cheaper, and more durable, paving the way for the huge electronic advances that were to follow.

BIRTH OF THE MICROCHIP

In the 1970s, the invention of the microchip, which contained thousands of tiny transistors on a piece of material smaller than a stamp, allowed complex circuits to be squeezed into a tiny space. This made the home computer possible. More recently, very large-scale integration (VLSI) has enabled hundreds of millions of transistors to be put on a single chip, meaning that even smaller computers can be made.

ELECTRONICS TODAY

Electronics is now part of virtually all electrical devices. The microprocessor, a complex circuit on a single chip, is used in devices from robots and space rockets to videocassette recorders (VCRs), telephones, and digital watches.

HOW A DIGITAL WATCH WORKS

A digital watch is powered by a battery. Its timing is controlled by a quartz crystal, which vibrates thousands of times a second. The microchip uses these vibrations to keep time, which it displays in numbers.

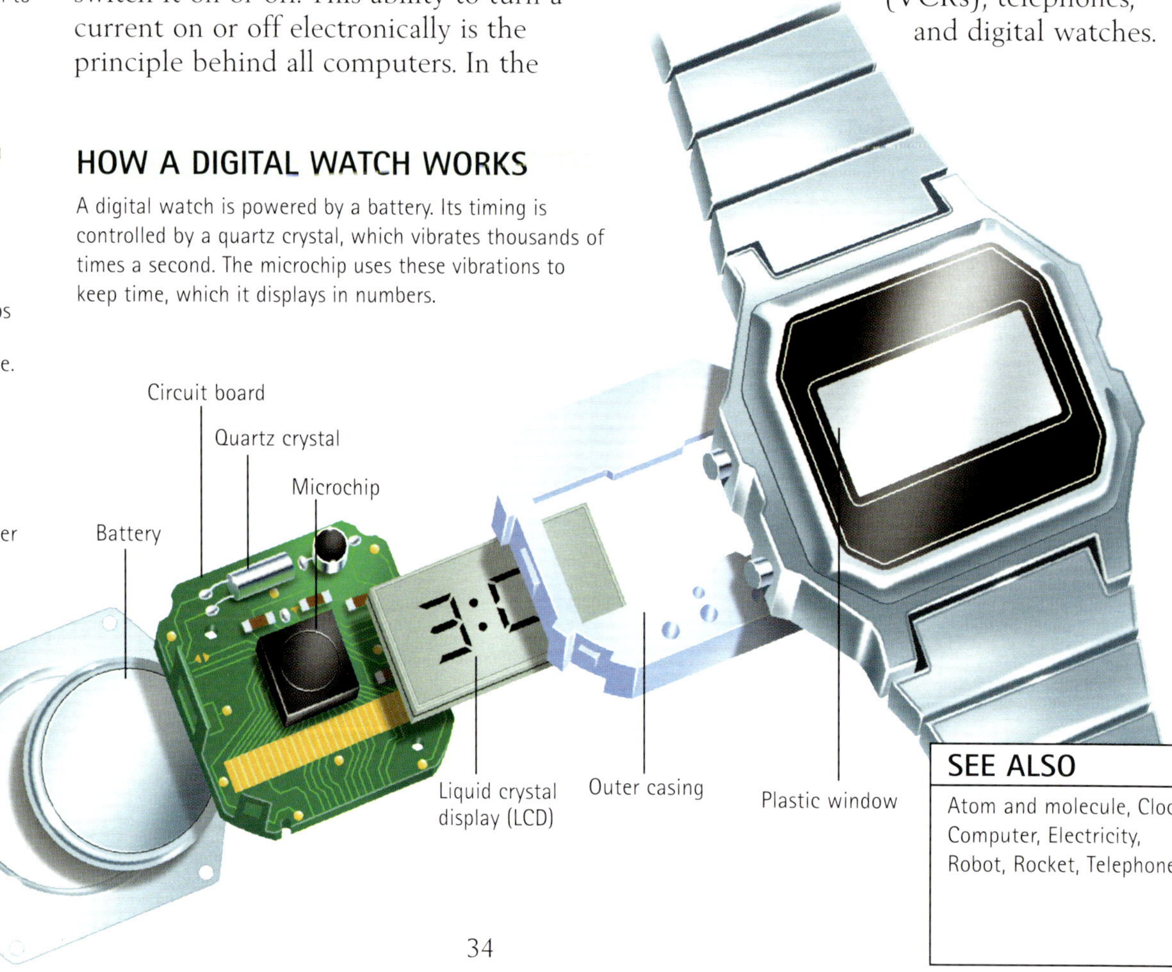

SEE ALSO

Atom and molecule, Clock, Computer, Electricity, Robot, Rocket, Telephone

Elephant

Elephants are the largest animals on land. They have very thick skin, a trunk, and ivory tusks. There are two species of elephant: the African and the Asian.

Asian elephants are the smaller type, growing to 10 ft. (3m) at the shoulder and weighing up to 5 tons.

African elephants are the largest land animals. They can reach 13 ft. (4m) and weigh up to 6 tons.

The African elephant lives in forests and open grassland and is the largest living land animal. The Asian or Indian elephant is mainly a forest animal. It is also smaller, with smaller ears, a more rounded back, and a trunk that ends in one fingerlike tip, instead of two.

EATING MACHINES

Elephants live on leaves and bark, eating up to 440 lb. (200kg) of food a day. They use their trunks, which are giant, flexible nostrils, to pull up plants and to bring food and water to their mouths. They have 12 back teeth (molars), but only 4 are fully developed and in use at any one time. All elephants have tusks, or extra long, curved teeth, which they use to strip bark off trees and to dig for water.

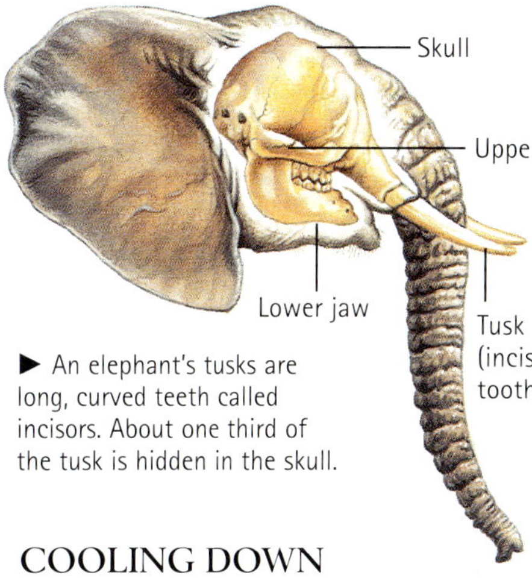

► An elephant's tusks are long, curved teeth called incisors. About one third of the tusk is hidden in the skull.

COOLING DOWN

Because elephants have no sweat glands, they lose very little body heat. They cool down by hiding in the shade and flapping their ears, or by bathing in water and using their trunks to shower themselves.

OLD AGE

All elephants, except the old bull males, are sociable animals and live in herds led by the oldest females. They can live for over 60 years, but many are killed for their ivory tusks. In many places the bull elephants, which have the biggest tusks, have become rare. The spread of human settlements has also led to both Asian and African elephants becoming endangered.

PROTECTIVE INSTINCTS

Female elephants start to breed when they are about ten years of age. They are pregnant for 20 months, before giving birth to a single calf. When a calf is about to be born, other females gather around the mother and the herd stays in one place until the young calf, which stands nearly 3 ft. (1m) tall, is on its feet and ready to move on.

SEE ALSO

Africa, Animal, Indian subcontinent, Mammal

Empire

An empire is a group of nations or states under the control of a single power. Most empires are built up when one country conquers others.

BRITISH INDIA
Over 600 small states, ruled by leaders including rajahs and maharajahs, came under the British Empire. They had their own laws, armies, and finances, but there were British troops in some states to guarantee loyalty.

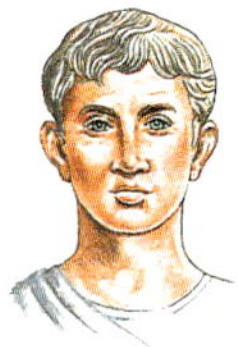

Octavian, later called Augustus, became the first emperor of Rome in 27 B.C.

From A.D. 527 to 565, Justinian ruled the Byzantine Empire with his wife.

In 1525, Babar founded the Mughal Empire by conquering northern India.

Süleyman enlarged the Ottoman Empire in the 1500s.

Maria Theresa and Francis I unified the Hapsburg Empire in the 1740s.

Haile Selassie, emperor of Ethiopia, was overthrown by the army in 1974.

Some of the greatest empires in history were the Roman, British, Byzantine, Japanese, Ottoman, and Russian empires. Each was ruled by an emperor or empress, but there have been other types of rule.

POWER GROWTH

Empires are usually built up when a country becomes richer or has larger armed forces than its neighbors, allowing it to spread its power and influence. The Greek king Alexander the Great trained his army with new weapons and tactics before conquering a vast empire from 334 to 323 B.C. The European Hapsburg dynasty used royal marriages and treaties to expand its Holy Roman Empire for more than 300 years from the 1400s. In the 1800s, the British Empire was won by economic strength, backed up by military superiority when needed.

IMPERIAL RULE

Many empires are ruled by a single state or nation, often with great brutality. The Assyrians in the ancient Middle East used their army to enforce the king's rule and to collect taxes. Those who disobeyed were cruelly punished. The Mongol Empire was run as a dictatorship in which the khan's wishes were enforced by the army. Other empires allowed some freedoms to their subjects. The states in the Athenian Empire of the 400s B.C. met each year to discuss events. Many of the cities and states in the Holy Roman Empire were free to run their own affairs, make their own laws, and even go to war.

KEY DATES

1500–1100 B.C. Egyptian New Kingdom rules an empire in southwest Asia

850–609 B.C. Assyria rules the Middle East

559–326 B.C. Persian Empire flourishes

264 B.C.–A.D. 410 Rome expands to rule vast areas before falling to barbarian invasion

228 B.C. China united under the Qin Dynasty

A.D. 800 Holy Roman Empire begins with the coronation of Charlemagne

1206 Genghis Khan founds the Mongol Empire

1492–1828 Spain conquers an empire in the Americas before colonies win independence

1880–1950s European powers build empires in Africa and Asia, then grant colonies independence

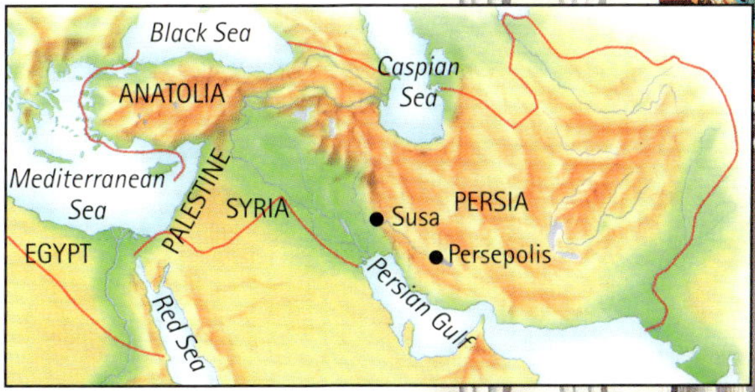

▲ The great palace of Persepolis was the center of the Persian Empire, founded by Darius the Great in 559 B.C. Nations subject to the Persian "King of Kings" brought tributes to Persepolis each spring as part of a great festival.

COLONIAL ADVENTURES

The Industrial Revolution made European states richer and better armed than other peoples. By 1850, several European nations owned colonies in Africa and Asia, which produced wealth and trade. In 1882, the British took over Egypt, prompting other European nations to conquer vast areas of Africa, Asia, and the Pacific and turn them into colonies. Within 40 years, it became clear that these colonies produced little wealth and were costly to maintain.

COLLAPSE OF EMPIRES

Empires may collapse as the result of foreign attack, member states breaking away, or internal dispute. The ancient Persian Empire was defeated in war by the Greeks under Alexander the Great. The Roman Empire was weakened by internal power struggles, and then fell to barbarian attacks during the 400s. In 1917, the German and Hapsburg empires were divided up into smaller states by the victorious Allies at the end of World War I, and the new states were racked by revolution, bringing an end to their empires.

A POSTIMPERIAL WORLD

Since 1945, very few empires have continued to exist. The colonial empires of the British, French, and other European nations broke up when, weakened by World War II, they could not afford to keep the colonies in the face of nationalist independence movements. In 1990, the Soviet Union broke up, as the states of the old Russian Empire declared themselves independent. There are few multinational empires in the world today, because most nations are able to survive economically, and do not need to be part of an empire to be protected from invaders.

▲ The Forbidden City, inside the city of Beijing, includes palaces of the Chinese emperors from 1421 to 1911. They are now preserved as museums and galleries.

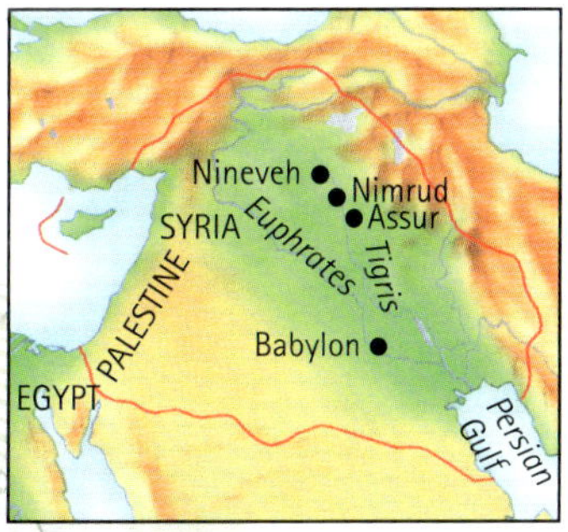

◀ The Assyrian Empire, with its capital at Nineveh, was a military state based on cruel and constant warfare. It collapsed in 609 B.C. when its enemies united to capture Nineveh.

SEE ALSO

Aztec, Babylon, Inca, Mongol Empire, Napoleonic Wars, Roman Empire

ENERGY

Energy is the ability to do work. An object or substance has energy if it can move or if it can generate such things as heat, sound, or electricity.

The Sun provides most of the heat and light energy that we use on Earth.

When anything, including a car, moves, it is using kinetic energy.

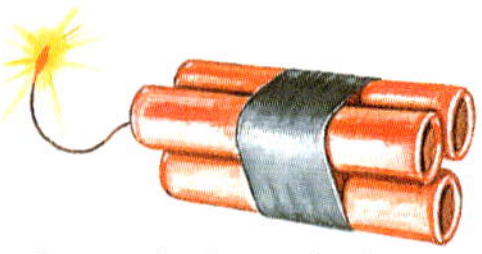

Dynamite's explosive power comes from stored chemical energy.

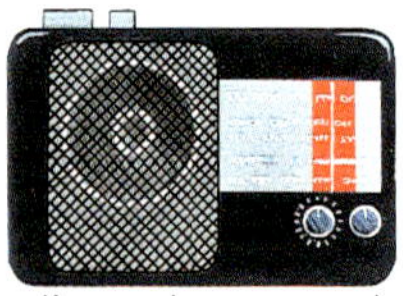

A radio produces sound energy by making the atoms in the air vibrate.

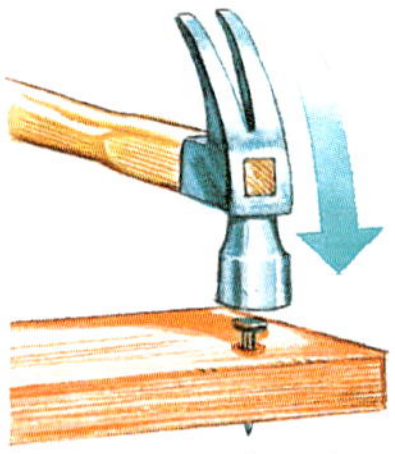

A hammer coming down to strike a nail uses the potential energy of gravity.

Nuclear energy takes its most dramatic form in a nuclear explosion.

Energy is everywhere—in sunlight as heat and light energy, in a CD player as sound energy, even in a lump of coal as stored chemical energy. Energy can be converted from one form into another, but it can never be destroyed.

MOVING OBJECTS

One of the most basic forms of energy is the energy of movement, or kinetic energy. Heavy, fast-moving objects have more kinetic energy than light, slow-moving ones. The kinetic energy of a car, for example, is less than that of a truck traveling at the same speed. A parked car has no kinetic energy at all.

HEAT ENERGY

Kinetic energy is also closely related to heat energy. An object is hot because its atoms (the tiny particles that it is made of) are constantly in motion. So an object's heat energy can be thought of as the kinetic energy of its atoms. The faster its atoms move, the hotter the object becomes.

SAVING IT FOR LATER

Energy can be stored to be used later. This energy in storage is called potential energy. A spring stores energy as it is squeezed. When it is released and expands back to its original shape, the potential energy becomes motion (kinetic energy). A diver crouched on a springboard also has potential energy that is converted when he or she jumps.

▲ A runner waiting on the blocks to start a race is like a coiled spring ready to expand. When the starter's gun goes off, the potential (stored) energy in her muscles is converted into the kinetic (motion) energy of running.

CHANGING FORM

The law of conservation of energy says that energy can never be destroyed or lost, but will change its form. For example, if a girl gliding on a pair of roller skates slowly comes to a halt, her kinetic energy gradually decreases to zero. But the energy does not vanish, it is transformed into two other energy forms: heat and sound. The heat, created by the friction of the roller-skate wheels rubbing on the ground, warms up both the wheels and the ground. The sound energy can be heard as a swish or squeak of the wheels.

AN ENERGETIC GAME OF PINBALL

Energy is constantly changing its state. In a game of pinball, potential energy is converted into kinetic energy. The moving ball will tend to slow down through friction as it comes into contact with parts of the machine. Energy is used up in overcoming friction, but it is not lost—it is changed into heat. When the player adds energy to the ball, by pushing it with a flipper, the ball speeds up.

1 Pulling back the plunger coils a spring just behind the ball. In energy terms, the potential energy in the player's hand is transferred to the spring.

ENERGY AND POWER

Scientists measure energy using units called joules (J). Power—the rate at which energy is used—is measured in watts (W). The idea of power involves time. If two hotpots heat a pint of water from 50°F (10°C) to 212°F (100°C), they both give the water the same amount of heat energy. But if one hotpot does the job in half the time, it has twice the amount of power as the other. Nuclear power works by releasing the energy locked inside the nucleus of an atom and using it to do work.

MAKING IT WORK

Energy is never lost, but it can be wasted if not put to work. Heat is the main cause of energy wastage. For example, an ordinary lightbulb converts only one fifth of its electrical energy into light; the rest is wasted as heat. Inefficiency of car engines also means that the Earth's natural energy resources, such as oil, are constantly being wasted.

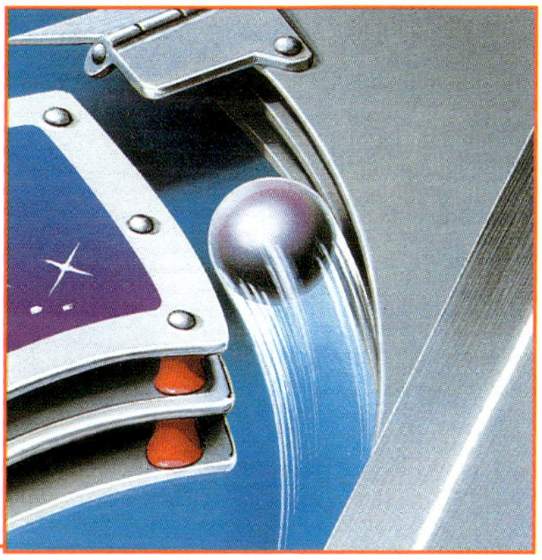

2 Letting go of the plunger shoots the ball into play. The spring's potential energy is changed into the kinetic energy of the moving ball.

3 As the ball moves inside the machine, it starts to slow down—its kinetic energy is being changed, mainly into heat. Flippers and obstacles have springs to speed up the ball.

ENERGY CYCLE

The Sun is our main source of energy on Earth. Every time it is used, the energy changes form. Other natural sources include oil, gas, and coal, but we use them wastefully.

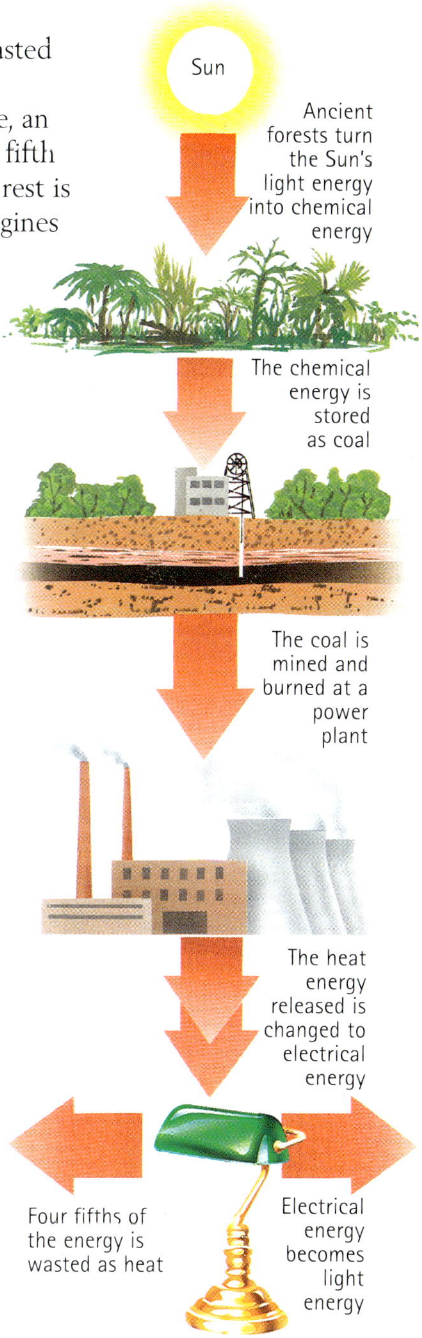

SEE ALSO

Ecology, Electricity, Force and motion, Heat, Light, Magnetism, Nuclear power, Solar power, Sound

Engine

Engines are machines which convert energy into mechanical work to power vehicles, drive other machines, or generate electricity.

FRANK WHITTLE
(1907–87) An officer in the British Royal Air Force, he designed the turbojet engine in 1941.

WERNHER VON BRAUN
(1912–77) Head of the team of German scientists during World War II that created the V2: the first rocket-powered guided missile, and the inspiration for later moon rockets.

The main types of engine are steam, gasoline (gas), diesel, jet, and rocket. Each one gets energy by burning, or combusting, fuels such as coal, gas, and diesel oil. Nearly all engines are internal combustion engines, which means the fuel is burned inside the engine, except the steam engine, which uses external combustion.

EARLY STEAM ENGINES

In the 1700s, much of the power for the Industrial Revolution was provided by the steam engine. In 1712, Englishman Thomas Newcomen developed the first practical steam engine for pumping water from mines. In 1765, a Scottish engineer, James Watt, began to improve the Newcomen steam engine and developed a much more efficient machine. Soon steam engines were powering factory machinery, as well as railroad cars, such as the *Rocket* locomotive, built by English engineer George Stephenson in 1829.

THE POWER OF STEAM

In a steam engine, a fire is used to boil water to produce high-pressure steam. As the steam expands, it pushes a piston back and forth in a cylinder, or turns the blades of a fanlike wheel called a turbine. These then drive the machine. Most steam engines have been replaced by internal combustion engines. However, many power plant generators today are still worked by steam turbines.

▲ An ultralight is a hang glider with an engine. It uses a two-stroke engine, which is lighter, cheaper, and more powerful for its size than a four-stroke engine.

GASOLINE ENGINES

Nowadays, cars, trucks, buses, and many trains and aircraft use internal combustion engines fueled by diesel oil or gas. In a gas engine, the fuel mixes with air inside a cylinder, and a spark sets the mixture on fire, pushing the piston up and down in a four-stroke cycle (see next page).

DIESEL ENGINES

Like gas engines, diesel engines have cylinders, pistons, valves, and a fuel supply, but there are no spark plugs or ignition system. The fuel explodes because of the heat created when the piston compresses the fuel and air inside a cylinder. The explosion pushes the piston up and down, which powers the vehicle.

STEAM LOCOMOTIVE

Steam locomotives powered the world's railroads for over 130 years. Hot gases from the burning coal surround the water tubes, turning the water to steam. The steam passes to the cylinder, driving the piston backward and forward. The piston pushes the connecting rod backward and forward, which rotates a crank and drives the wheels. Water and coal are carried in the tender.

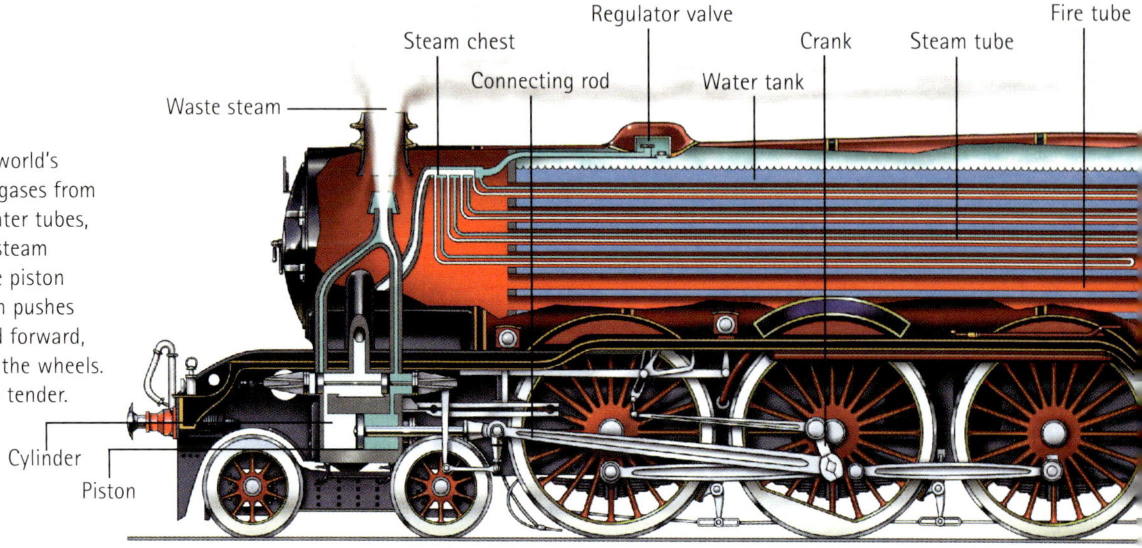

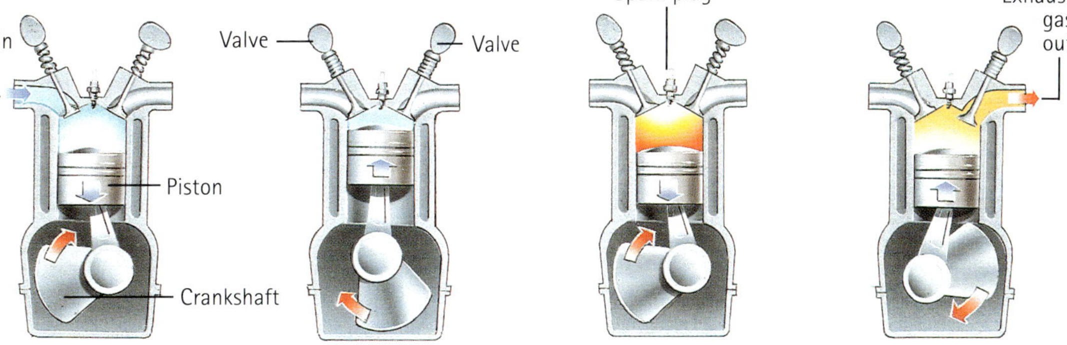

A FOUR-STROKE ENGINE
Cars have internal combustion engines with pistons that work in a four-stroke cycle (the piston makes two movements up and two down). Air and fuel are let into the piston cylinder by valves at the top. The explosion of ignited fuel moves the piston, which turns a crankshaft. This spins the driveshaft (a rod connected to the wheels via the gearbox).

1 **Induction.** As the piston goes down, it draws a mixture of air and fuel into the cylinder.

2 **Compression.** The piston rises, compressing the air and fuel mixture ready for ignition.

3 **Power.** A spark lights the fuel, forcing the piston down and turning the crankshaft.

4 **Exhaust.** On the final stroke of the engine, the piston rises to expel exhaust (waste) gases.

THE GAS TURBINE

A jet, or gas turbine, engine does not have pistons. Instead, air is sucked in at the front of the engine and compressed, or squashed, by the rotating blades of the compressor. The air is then blown into the combustion chamber, where it is ignited with aviation fuel. The hot gases created are expelled from the back of the engine, pushing the plane forward.

TO THE STARS

Like jet engines, rocket engines also use their exhaust gases to push the vehicle forward. Unlike jets, however, rockets cannot burn fuel by taking in oxygen from the air, since there is no air in space. Instead, they carry their oxygen supply with them, usually as liquid oxygen. The fuel either ignites spontaneously when mixed with the oxygen, or is lit by a spark.

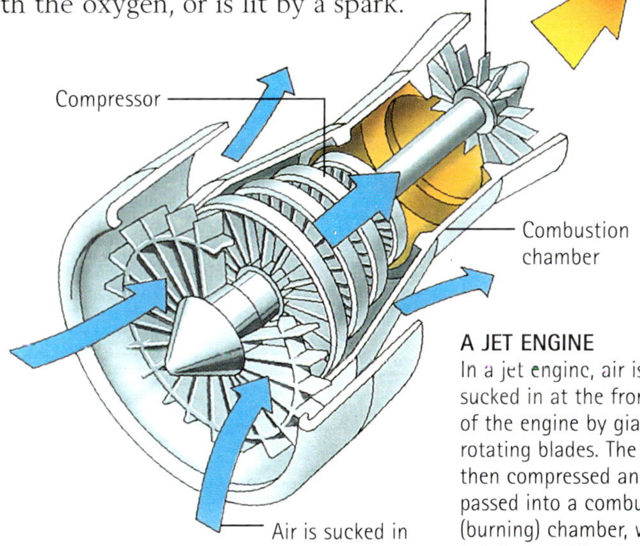

A JET ENGINE
In a jet engine, air is sucked in at the front of the engine by giant rotating blades. The air is then compressed and passed into a combustion (burning) chamber, where it is ignited. The plane is thrust forward by the exhaust gases. These gases also turn a turbine, which drives the compressor.

KEY DATES

1862	Alphonse Beau de Rochas invents the four-stroke cycle
1876	Nikolaus Otto develops the prototype automobile engine
1878	Sir Dougald Clerk invents the two-stroke cycle
1892	Rudolph Diesel patents the diesel engine
1897	C. P. Steinmetz's *Future of Electricity* predicts air pollution from use of coal as fuel
1939	The first jet-engined aircraft, the Heinkel, flies in Germany
1944	The first V2 missile is fired on enemy targets

The tender holds a supply of coal for the fire, which turns the water into steam

SEE ALSO
Aircraft, Car, Electricity, Energy, Rocket, Train, Transportation

EUROPE

Europe is the second smallest of the world's seven continents. It has 45 countries, including parts of Russia, Turkey, and Kazakhstan.

KEY FACTS

- **Area:** 4,032,075 sq. mi.
- **Population:** 713,133,000
- **Number of countries:** 45
- **Largest country:** Russia, 25 percent of which (1,663,872 sq. mi.) is in Europe
- **Smallest country:** Vatican City (0.17 sq. mi.)
- **Highest point:** Mount Elbrus (18,481 ft.)
- **Largest lake:** Lake Ladoga (7,000 sq. mi.)
- **Longest river:** Volga (2,325 sq. mi.)

Only the continent of Australia is smaller than Europe, but Europe's moderate climate, rich resources, and fertile land support a large population. Between them, the people speak about 50 languages and many more dialects. With its 45 countries, Europe is a continent of diverse cultures.

NEVER FAR FROM WATER

The northwest and west of Europe are bordered by the Arctic and Atlantic oceans, and the Mediterranean Sea surrounds the south. The coastline is broken up by thousands of fjords and other inlets, and only nine European countries have no access to the sea.

NORTH EUROPEAN PLAIN

Many of Europe's most populated areas lie on the North European Plain, which stretches from the southern part of the United Kingdom through northern France, Germany, and Poland to the Ural Mountains in Russia. To the north are forests of coniferous trees such as fir, larch, and pine. Deciduous forests of ash, elm, and oak grow in central and southern Europe. In the southeast are large areas of dry grassland called steppes.

▲ Iceland in the North Atlantic Ocean is known as the "Land of Ice and Fire" because of its volcanoes and hot springs set against a landscape of ice fields and glaciers.

SCANDINAVIA

In the far north of Europe lies the cold and mountainous region of Scandinavia, which includes the countries of Norway, Sweden, Denmark, and Finland. The climate around the Arctic Ocean is cold and snowy, with temperatures in January averaging below 3°F (–16°C). Few trees grow in the extreme north, but the forests farther south contain large animals such as brown bears, reindeer, and wolves.

▼ Wine is produced throughout Europe, particularly in France (shown here), Germany, Spain, Italy, and Bulgaria.

KEY TO MAP
1 THE NETHERLANDS
2 BELGIUM
3 LUXEMBOURG
4 SWITZERLAND
5 LIECHTENSTEIN
6 MONACO
7 ANDORRA
8 VATICAN CITY
9 SAN MARINO
10 SLOVENIA
11 CROATIA
12 BOSNIA-HERZEGOVINA
13 YUGOSLAVIA
14 MACEDONIA
15 ALBANIA
16 MOLDOVA

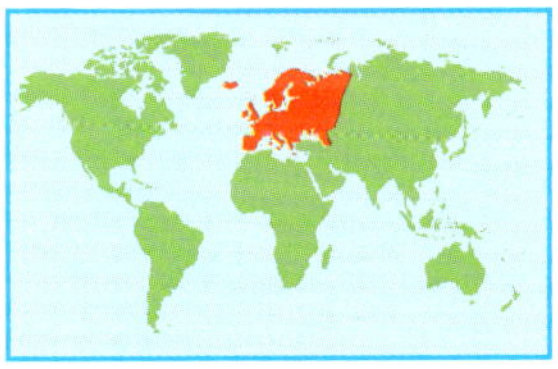

THE MEDITERRANEAN

The southern part of Europe is divided from the north by three mountain ranges: the Pyrenees, the Alps, and the Carpathian Mountains. The Mediterranean countries of southern Europe, including Italy, Spain, and Greece, have mild, rainy winters and hot, dry summers.

A FERTILE CONTINENT

Europe is a fertile continent; farms cover more than half the land. Crops include barley, oats, potatoes, and wheat, and citrus fruits and olives in the south. Vast areas of steppe in the Ukraine and southern Russia are heavily farmed for grain.

OIL, GAS, AND COAL

Oil and natural gas are produced in the North Sea, and coal is found in large quantities in Europe. These fuels help power the continent's many factories—Europe produces more manufactured goods than any other continent, including cars, electronic goods, ships, and steel.

A MIXED POPULATION

Most Europeans are the descendants of people who lived on the continent in prehistoric times, but there is a long history of immigration from Africa, Asia, and the Caribbean. About 70 percent of the population lives in cities and towns, working in factories or service industries, such as finance and tourism. ▶

▲ The number of red squirrels has decreased in Europe in the 1900s, following the introduction of the gray squirrel from North America and loss of large areas of woodland.

▲ Istanbul in Turkey lies on the shores of the Bosporus, the strait that divides Europe from Asia. Its buildings reflect a mixture of Eastern and Western styles.

BRANCHES OF CHRISTIANITY

Christianity is Europe's leading religion. Many follow the Roman Catholic Church, which has its headquarters in Vatican City, in Rome, Italy. Protestantism is a branch of Christianity with its highest European representation in the north of the continent. The Orthodox Church flourishes in the east and southeast.

HISTORICAL CITIES

Many of Europe's large cities are steeped in history, but are also characterized by modern architecture and a modern way of life. Paris in France contains magnificent buildings dating from the Middle Ages, and is at the same time a leading fashion center. Moscow in Russia and London in England are important international cities, as well as historic sites. Athens and Rome, the capitals of Greece and Italy, have impressive ruins surviving from the days of Ancient Greece and the Roman Empire.

DEMOCRACY AND LAW

Throughout history, Europe has had an important influence on world politics. The system of democracy—where the government is chosen by the people—was first tried in Ancient Greece about 2,500 years ago. Similarly, many of the laws developed during the Roman civilization (from 590 B.C. to A.D. 476) still influence legal systems today.

▲ The ruins of Delphi, a sacred site from as early as 1100 B.C., stand on Mount Parnassus in the southern part of mainland Greece.

THE RENAISSANCE

From the 1300s, Europe became an increasingly important center of art and learning, with people interested in new ideas about art, science, and literature. This period is known as the Renaissance. At the same time, a desire for trade led European seafarers to set out to explore unknown lands and later to start colonies abroad. In the late 1700s, the continent was the birthplace of the Industrial Revolution, which brought great power and prosperity to the West.

END OF EMPIRES

The map of Europe has often changed throughout history, largely because of wars between rival countries. In the 1900s, two great world wars were fought between European powers. In the years following World War II (1939–45), the empires created in Africa and Asia by European countries such as Belgium, Britain, France,

◀ Many European countries, including Germany, the Netherlands, Romania, and Italy, have strong national soccer teams and attract enthusiastic fans, like these from Switzerland.

the Netherlands, and Portugal came to an end. Former colonies became independent countries, but many people living there continued to follow European customs and speak European languages. A large number of them have since made their homes in Europe.

▲ After World War II, about a seventh of Berlin was in ruins. The city was divided between East and West until 1990, when Germany was reunited.

EAST AND WEST

By the 1950s, Europe was divided between the noncommunist countries of the West and the Soviet-backed communist countries of the East. Until the 1980s, the two sides remained armed and hostile throughout the period known as the Cold War. But from the late 1980s, the Eastern European countries threw off their communist governments following the breakup of the Soviet Union in 1991. Yugoslavia also split up into five separate countries at this time, and a new map of Europe took shape, with new countries and partnerships. Today's Europe enjoys greater cooperation than at any other time during the 1900s.

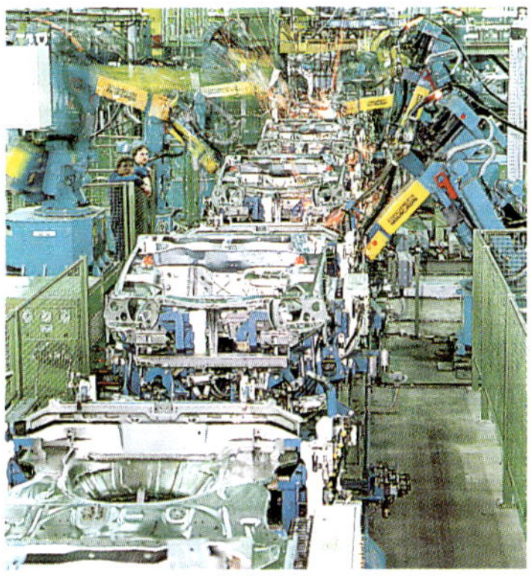

◀ German car-making factories are among the most highly automated in the world, and the cars they produce are exported worldwide.

THE EUROPEAN UNION

In the 1950s, a group of countries in Western Europe set up the European Community, or Common Market, to encourage greater economic unity in Europe. Over the years, the Community grew into the European Union, with 15 member countries aiming not only for greater economic cooperation, but also greater political unity.

SEE ALSO

Eastern Europe, France, Germany, Greece and the Balkans, Italy, Netherlands, Belgium, and Luxembourg, Scandinavia, Spain and Portugal, Switzerland and Austria, United Kingdom

EVOLUTION

Evolution is the way in which an organism changes over many generations, resulting in a species that is very different from its early ancestors.

THE HORSE

Today's hoofed horse evolved over millions of years from an animal the size of a dog.

Hyracotherium (55–40 million years ago [mya]) was 10 in. (25cm) tall, with four toes.

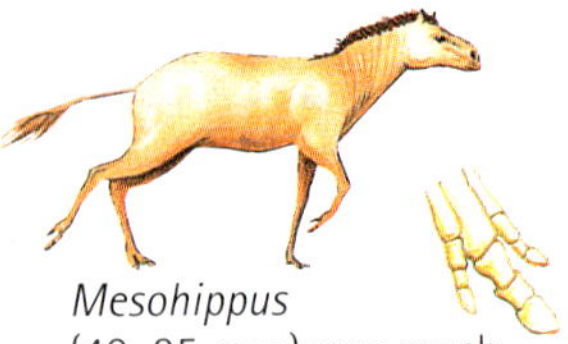

Mesohippus (40–25 mya) was much larger and had three toes.

Merychippus (25–5 mya) was better suited to firm, grassy plains.

Pliohippus (5–2 mya) had stronger legs and single hooves.

Equus caballus (1.5 mya) was similar to today's horse.

Most scientists believe that the first simple organisms appeared on Earth over three billion years ago, and that all today's plants and animals have arisen from these by a process of gradual change. This process, which is constantly happening from one generation to the next, is known as evolution.

DARWIN'S THEORY

The idea of evolution has been around since the age of the Ancient Greeks. However, the first convincing theory of how evolution works was provided in the mid-1800s by the English naturalist Charles Darwin. Darwin saw that plants and animals produce lots of offspring, but that only a small number survive. Darwin concluded that only the individual with the most useful features can survive in what he called the struggle for existence.

SURVIVAL OF THE FITTEST

Individuals that are not suited to their surroundings die out, leaving only the fittest ones to breed and pass the useful features on to their offspring. In popular terms, this process is known as "survival of the fittest." It explains the great variety of plant and animal life throughout the world—because conditions vary from place to place, so animals adapt to fit.

EVOLUTION FACTS AND FIGURES

- Scientists estimate that 99.9 percent of all the species that have ever lived are now extinct
- The idea of evolution was first suggested by the Ancient Greeks more than 2,500 years ago
- Another naturalist called Alfred Wallace came up with the same theory of evolution as Darwin (and at the same time), but Darwin published his ideas first
- By looking at fossilized animals in different layers of rock, scientists can see how the animals evolved
- When Darwin visited the Galapagos Islands he saw that all the finches had different beaks to suit their food, such as a long, hooked beak for catching insects or a nutcracker-shaped beak for eating seeds

THE MARCH OF TIME

All life-forms probably developed from single-celled sea organisms. From there, evolution branched out in different directions. One group of fish, for example, evolved into amphibians, and one group of amphibians then gave rise to the reptiles. Birds and mammals evolved from different groups of reptiles. *Archaeopteryx* lived about 150 million years ago. It had wings and feathers and was obviously a bird, but its teeth were reptilian, indicating that it was in an evolutionary stage between the two.

▲ Hungry Dutch explorers on the island of Mauritius in the 1500s were new predators for the trusting flightless dodo, extinct by 1680.

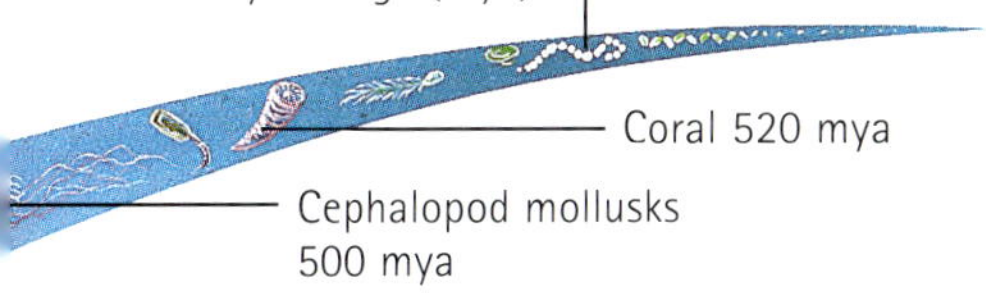

LITTLE BY LITTLE

With each new generation, the struggle for existence continues, with the result that plants and animals gradually change and become better adapted to their surroundings. Each change may be almost invisible, but over millions of years they all make a great difference.

NATURAL SELECTION

Conditions are not the same everywhere, so a variation that is useful in one area might be less useful in another. A species that spreads out may therefore evolve, or change, over a long time into several different species. Because this process of weeding out the inefficient individuals and favoring the fittest ones is an entirely natural one, Darwin gave it the name natural selection.

EVIDENCE FROM THE ROCKS

Some of the strongest support for the idea of evolution comes from the fossilized remains of plants and animals found in rocks formed from layers of sand and mud on ancient seabeds. In each layer of rock, the organisms look slightly different from the ones below, suggesting a process of change over time.

A COMMON ANCESTOR

The bone structure of living animals also gives clues to evolution. A human's arm, a bird's wing, and a whale's flipper all look very different and have different uses, but their bones are very similar. This suggests that these animals have all evolved from a common ancestor, which spread out over a wide area, allowing its arms to be adapted for different jobs.

CHARLES DARWIN (1809–1882) shook the world, and especially the Church, with his theory of natural selection, which he published in *On the Origin of Species* in 1859.

JEAN BAPTISTE LAMARCK (1744–1829) was a French biologist who believed that animals evolved during their own lifetimes. For example, each giraffe, by stretching, elongated its neck.

SEE ALSO

Dinosaur, Fossil, Genetics, Horse, Prehistoric animal, Prehistoric people

EXPLORER

People explore to discover the unknown. Through exploration we have learned much about the Earth. We are still exploring the oceans and outer space.

Christopher Columbus opened up America to European trade in 1492.

Captain Robert Scott died on the way back from the South Pole in 1912.

Jacques Cousteau helped invent the aqualung so he could explore under water.

The Phoenicians were among the first explorers, sailing the Mediterranean around 3,000 years ago. Pytheas, a Greek sailor, ventured into the Atlantic Ocean in 300 B.C. and, in A.D. 1000, Norway's Leif Ericsson reached North America.

THE SILK ROAD

Chinese and Arab travelers made long overland journeys. In 138 B.C., Zhang Qian became the first Chinese man to explore central Asia. Later, European merchants took the Silk Road to China, visited by the Italian Marco Polo in 1275 and described in his book *Description of the World*.

AGE OF DISCOVERY

In the 1400s, stronger ships and the invention of navigational aids such as the backstaff (used to plot the ship's position by the Sun and stars) prompted European explorers to head to sea. They went in search of lands to conquer and for trade, riches, and slaves. Seeking a sea route to India, Portuguese sailors headed south along the African coast. In 1488, Bartholomeu Días reached the southern tip of Africa, and in 1498, Vasco da Gama crossed the Indian Ocean. Columbus arrived in America from Spain in 1492.

MAPMAKERS

In 1522, Ferdinand Magellan's ship from Spain completed the first voyage around the world. He died on the way, but the trip proved that the Earth was round. In the 1770s, James Cook of the British navy sailed the Pacific, mapping the coast of New Zealand and landing in Australia.

LAST FRONTIERS

Later explorers moved inland. The Scottish missionary David Livingstone traveled into Africa. Robert Peary of the United States conquered the North Pole in 1909, and Norway's Roald Amundsen reached the South Pole in 1911. In 1960, the *Trieste* dived 35,800 ft. (10,910m) under the sea, and in 1969 a human being walked on the Moon.

INTO THE UNKNOWN

Early sea voyages advanced navigational knowledge and helped mapmakers to produce more accurate maps. In the 1400s, Prince Henry the Navigator, of Portugal, skilled in mathematics and astronomy, helped organize 50 expeditions to West Africa. These trips pushed back the frontiers of navigation and paved the way for future trade and navigation.

SEE ALSO

Antarctica, Asia, Australia, Map, Ocean and sea, Space exploration, Submarine, Viking

Propelled by rocket engines, the supersonic X-15 holds the world air-speed record at 4,520 mph set in 1967.

The funeral mask of the pharaoh Tutankhamen was found in his tomb, discovered in 1922.

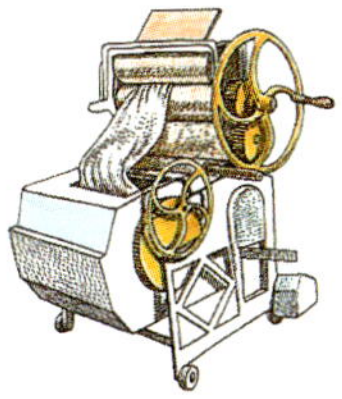

The first washing machine (invented by Hamilton Smith, U.S.A., 1858) still relied on muscle power.

On April 12, 1961, Yuri Gagarin of the U.S.S.R. became the first person in space onboard *Vostok 1*.

The steam gun carriage of 1769, invented by French engineer Cugnot, was the first motorized vehicle.

FACTFINDER

Whether for school projects, or just for fun, this section provides facts, figures, and other essential information—from a world map to presidents and states, and on to biographies of famous figures. It finishes with the highlights of the 20th century. Timelines present key international (top) and U.S. (bottom) developments.

The *chanoyu*, a Japanese tea ceremony which can last four hours, actually originated in China.

In 1834, Charles Babbage (1792-1871) designed the first mechanical computer, but he never saw it built.

The Venus flytrap is a carnivorous plant that feeds on the insects it traps in its leaves.

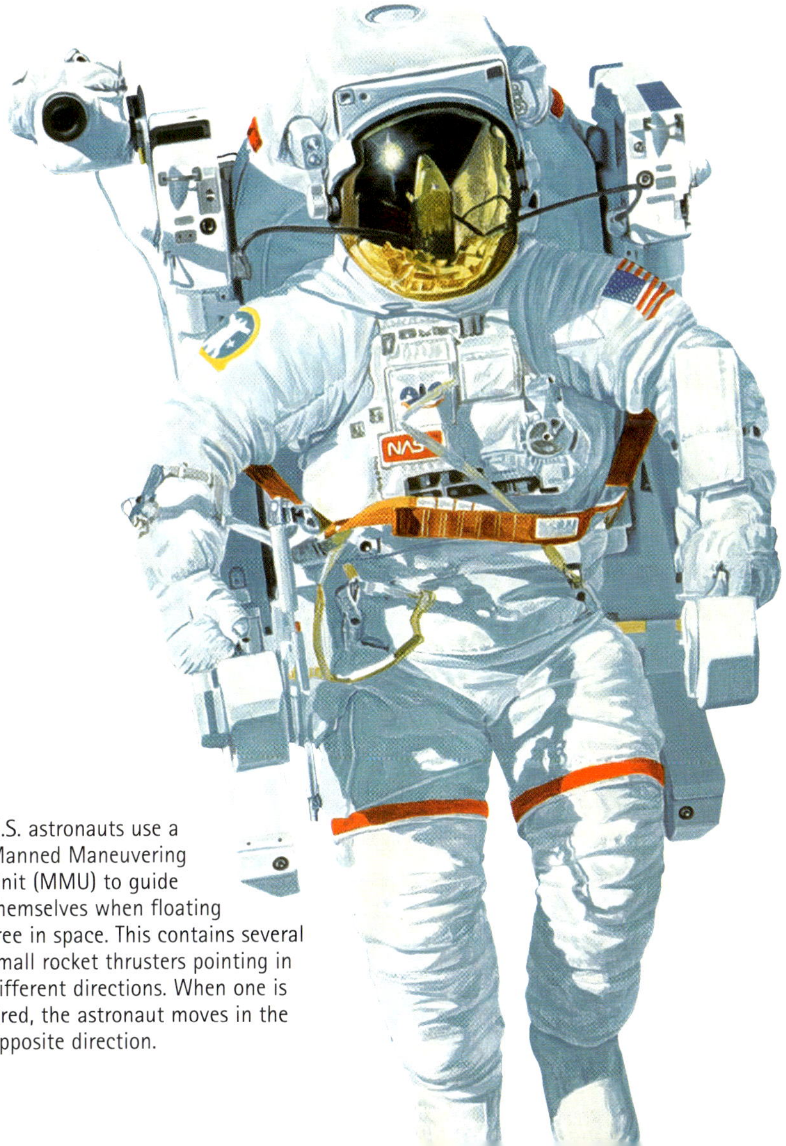

U.S. astronauts use a Manned Maneuvering Unit (MMU) to guide themselves when floating free in space. This contains several small rocket thrusters pointing in different directions. When one is fired, the astronaut moves in the opposite direction.

The Arctic tern is a long-distance flyer, making an annual round trip of up to 25,000 miles.

Camptosaurus was an ornithopod ("bird-footed") dinosaur that lived about 150 million years ago.

Edgar Allan Poe (1809-49) was one of America's greatest poets and an early writer of horror stories.

COUNTRIES OF THE WORLD

KEY TO MAP

1 NETHERLANDS
2 BELGIUM
3 LUXEMBOURG
4 SWITZERLAND
5 LIECHTENSTEIN
6 AUSTRIA
7 ANDORRA
8 MONACO
9 SAN MARINO
10 VATICAN CITY
11 CZECH REPUBLIC
12 SLOVAK REPUBLIC
13 SLOVENIA
14 CROATIA
15 BOSNIA-HERZEGOVINA
16 YUGOSLAVIA
17 MACEDONIA
18 ALBANIA
19 HUNGARY
20 MOLDOVA
21 ESTONIA
22 LATVIA
23 LITHUANIA
24 KALININGRAD (RUSSIA)
25 GEORGIA
26 AZERBAIJAN
27 ARMENIA
28 ANTIGUA AND BARBUDA
29 ST. KITTS AND NEVIS
30 DOMINICA
31 ST. LUCIA
32 ST. VINCENT AND THE GRENADINES
33 BARBADOS
34 GRENADA
35 TRINIDAD AND TOBAGO
36 EQUATORIAL GUINEA
37 SÃO TOMÉ AND PRÍNCIPE

miles
0
3,000
0
3,000
km
ARCTIC OCEAN
SWEDEN
FINLAND
RUSSIA
21
22
23
24
MARK
POLAND
BELARUS
UKRAINE
KAZAKHSTAN
MONGOLIA
NORTH PACIFIC OCEAN
11
12
6
20
19
ROMANIA
13
14
9
15
16
BULGARIA
17
18
10
25
26
27
UZBEKISTAN
KYRGYZSTAN
TURKMENISTAN
TAJIKISTAN
NORTH KOREA
SOUTH KOREA
JAPAN
GREECE
TURKEY
MALTA
CYPRUS
SYRIA
LEBANON
ISRAEL
JORDAN
IRAQ
IRAN
AFGHANISTAN
CHINA
KUWAIT
PAKISTAN
BHUTAN
NEPAL
LIBYA
EGYPT
BAHRAIN
QATAR
SAUDI ARABIA
UNITED ARAB EMIRATES
INDIA
BANGLADESH
MYANMAR (BURMA)
TAIWAN
LAOS
VIETNAM
THAILAND
CAMBODIA
OMAN
YEMEN
ERITREA
CHAD
SUDAN
DJIBOUTI
PHILIPPINES
ETHIOPIA
SOMALI REPUBLIC
CENTRAL AFRICAN REP.
SRI LANKA
MALDIVES
PALAU
FED. STATES OF MICRONESIA
MARSHALL IS.
KIRIBATI
MALAYSIA
UGANDA
KENYA
DEM. REP. OF CONGO
REP. OF CONGO
SINGAPORE
INDONESIA
NAURU
RWANDA
BURUNDI
TANZANIA
SEYCHELLES
PAPUA NEW GUINEA
TUVALU
SOLOMON IS.
ANGOLA
COMOROS
ZAMBIA
MALAWI
INDIAN OCEAN
WESTERN SAMOA
ZIMBABWE
MOZAMBIQUE
MAURITIUS
VANUATU
FIJI
NAMIBIA
MADAGASCAR
BOTSWANA
REUNION (Fr.)
NEW CALEDONIA (Fr.)
SWAZILAND
AUSTRALIA
SOUTH AFRICA
LESOTHO
NEW ZEALAND
ANTARCTICA

c. 9000 B.C.
Agriculture develops in Middle East

c. 3500 B.C.
First cities appear in Sumeria; writing invented

c. 3100 B.C.
Upper and Lower Egypt united

c. 2500 B.C.
Indus Valley civilization in Pakistan

2300s B.C.
Mesopotamia, world's first empire, flourishes

STATES OF THE UNITED STATES

STATE	CAPITAL	POPULATION (1997 ESTIMATE)	(RANK)	AREA (IN SQ. MI.)	(RANK)	ENTRY INTO UNION	(ORDER)
Alabama	Montgomery	4,319,000	(23)	52,423	(30)	December 14, 1819	(22)
Alaska	Juneau	609,000	(48)	656,424	(1)	January 3, 1959	(49)
Arizona	Phoenix	4,555,000	(21)	114,006	(6)	February 14, 1912	(48)
Arkansas	Little Rock	2,523,000	(33)	53,182	(29)	June 15, 1836	(25)
California	Sacramento	32,268,000	(1)	163,707	(3)	September 9, 1850	(31)
Colorado	Denver	3,893,000	(25)	104,100	(8)	August 1, 1876	(38)
Connecticut	Hartford	3270,000	(28)	5,544	(48)	January 9, 1788	(5)
Delaware	Dover	732,000	(46)	2,489	(49)	December 7, 1787	(1)
Florida	Tallahassee	14,654,000	(4)	65,758	(22)	March 3, 1845	(27)
Georgia	Atlanta	7,486,000	(10)	59,441	(24)	January 2, 1788	(4)
Hawaii	Honolulu	1,187,000	(41)	10,932	(43)	August 21, 1959	(50)
Idaho	Boise	1,210,000	(40)	83,574	(14)	July 3, 1890	(43)
Illinois	Springfield	11,896,000	(6)	57,918	(25)	December 3, 1818	(21)
Indiana	Indianapolis	5,864,000	(14)	36,420	(38)	December 11, 1816	(19)
Iowa	Des Moines	2,852,000	(30)	56,276	(26)	December 28, 1846	(29)
Kansas	Topeka	2,595,000	(32)	82,282	(15)	January 29, 1861	(34)
Kentucky	Frankfort	3,908,000	(24)	40,411	(37)	June 1, 1792	(15)
Louisiana	Baton Rouge	4,352,000	(22)	51,843	(31)	April 30, 1812	(18)
Maine	Augusta	1,242,000	(39)	35,387	(39)	March 15, 1820	(23)
Maryland	Annapolis	5,094,000	(19)	12,407	(42)	April 28, 1788	(7)
Massachusetts	Boston	6,118,000	(13)	10,555	(44)	February 6, 1788	(6)
Michigan	Lansing	9,774,000	(8)	96,705	(11)	January 26, 1837	(26)
Minnesota	St. Paul	4,686,000	(20)	86,943	(12)	May 11, 1858	(32)
Mississippi	Jackson	2,731,000	(31)	48,434	(32)	December 10, 1817	(20)
Missouri	Jefferson City	5,402,000	(16)	69,709	(21)	August 10, 1821	(24)
Montana	Helena	879,000	(44)	147,046	(4)	November 8, 1889	(41)
Nebraska	Lincoln	1,657,000	(38)	77,358	(16)	March 1, 1867	(37)
Nevada	Carson City	1,677,000	(37)	110,567	(7)	October 31, 1864	(36)
New Hampshire	Concord	1,173,000	(42)	9,351	(46)	June 21, 1788	(9)
New Jersey	Trenton	8,053,000	(9)	8,722	(47)	December 18, 1787	(3)
New Mexico	Santa Fe	1,730,000	(36)	121,598	(5)	January 6, 1912	(47)
New York	Albany	18,137,000	(3)	54,556	(27)	July 26, 1788	(11)
North Carolina	Raleigh	7,425,000	(11)	53,821	(28)	November 21, 1789	(12)
North Dakota	Bismarck	641,000	(47)	70,704	(19)	November 2, 1889	(39)
Ohio	Columbus	11,186,000	(7)	44,828	(34)	March 1, 1803	(17)
Oklahoma	Oklahoma City	3,317,000	(27)	69,903	(20)	November 16, 1907	(46)
Oregon	Salem	3,243,000	(29)	98,386	(9)	February 14, 1859	(33)
Pennsylvania	Harrisburg	12,020,000	(5)	46,058	(33)	December 12, 1787	(2)
Rhode Island	Providence	987,000	(43)	1,545	(50)	May 29, 1790	(13)
South Carolina	Columbia	3,760,000	(26)	32,008	(40)	May 23, 1788	(8)
South Dakota	Pierre	738,000	(45)	77,121	(17)	November 2, 1889	(40)
Tennessee	Nashville	5,368,000	(17)	42,146	(36)	June 1, 1796	(16)
Texas	Austin	19,439,000	(2)	268,601	(2)	December 29, 1845	(28)
Utah	Salt Lake City	2,059,000	(34)	84,904	(13)	January 4, 1896	(45)
Vermont	Montpelier	589,000	(49)	9,615	(45)	March 4, 1791	(14)
Virginia	Richmond	6,734,000	(12)	42,777	(35)	June 25, 1788	(10)
Washington	Olympia	5,610,000	(15)	71,302	(18)	November 11, 1889	(42)
West Virginia	Charleston	1,816,000	(35)	24,231	(41)	June 20, 1863	(35)
Wisconsin	Madison	5,170,000	(18)	65,499	(23)	May 29, 1848	(30)
Wyoming	Cheyenne	480,000	(50)	97,818	(10)	July 10, 1890	(44)

American Indian ancestors arrive from Asia
38 000 B.C.–8000 B.C.

Folsom culture in the Great Plains
9000 B.C.–8000 B.C.

Olmec civilization in Mexico and Central America
1200 B.C.–100 B.C.

Maya civilization in Central America
A.D. 300–900

Mound Builders in Mississippi Valley
700

Vikings explore NE coast of North America
1000

c. 1792–50 B.C.
King Hammurabi rules Babylonia

800–600 B.C.
Assyrian Empire

551 B.C.
Birth of Confucius

500–323 B.C.
Golden Age of Greece

563 B.C.
Birth of Buddha

331 B.C.
Alexander the Great conquers Persian Empire

PRESIDENTS OF THE UNITED STATES

	NAME (PARTY)*	BIRTH-DEATH DATES	TERM IN OFFICE	VICE PRESIDENT(S)
1.	George Washington *(F)*	1732 – 1799	Apr. 30, 1789 – Mar. 4, 1797	John Adams
2.	John Adams *(F)*	1735 – 1826	Mar. 4, 1797 – Mar. 4, 1801	Thomas Jefferson
3.	Thomas Jefferson *(D–R)*	1743 – 1826	Mar. 4, 1801 – Mar. 4, 1809	Aaron Burr George Clinton
4.	James Madison *(D–R)*	1751 – 1836	Mar. 4, 1809 – Mar. 4, 1817	George Clinton Elbridge Gerry
5.	James Monroe *(D–R)*	1758 – 1831	Mar. 4, 1817 – Mar. 4, 1825	Daniel D. Tompkins
6.	John Quincy Adams *(D–R)*	1767 – 1848	Mar. 4, 1825 – Mar. 4, 1829	John C. Calhoun
7.	Andrew Jackson *(D)*	1767 – 1845	Mar. 4, 1829 – Mar. 4, 1837	John C. Calhoun, Martin Van Buren
8.	Martin Van Buren *(D)*	1782 – 1862	Mar. 4, 1837 – Mar. 4, 1841	Richard M. Johnson
9.	William Henry Harrison *(W)*	1773 – 1841	Mar. 4, 1841 – Apr. 4, 1841	John Tyler
10.	John Tyler *(W)*	1790 – 1862	Apr. 4, 1841 – Mar. 4, 1845	–
11.	James K. Polk *(D)*	1795 – 1849	Mar. 4, 1845 – Mar. 4, 1849	George M. Dallas
12.	Zachary Taylor *(W)*	1784 – 1850	Mar. 4, 1849 – July 9, 1850	Millard Fillmore
13	Millard Fillmore *(W)*	1800 – 1874	July 9, 1850 – Mar. 4, 1853	–
14.	Franklin Pierce *(D)*	1804 – 1869	Mar. 4, 1853 – Mar. 4, 1857	William R. King
15.	James Buchanan *(D)*	1791 – 1868	Mar. 4, 1857 – Mar. 4, 1861	John C. Breckinridge
16.	Abraham Lincoln *(R)*	1809 – 1865	Mar. 4, 1861 – Apr. 15, 1865	Hannibal Hamlin, Andrew Johnson
17.	Andrew Johnson *(R)*	1808 – 1875	Apr. 15, 1865 – Mar. 4, 1869	–
18.	Ulysses S. Grant *(R)*	1822 – 1885	Mar. 4, 1869 – Mar. 4, 1877	Schuyler Colfax Henry Wilson
19.	Rutherford B. Hayes *(R)*	1822 – 1893	Mar. 4, 1877 – Mar. 4, 1881	William A. Wheeler
20.	James A. Garfield *(R)*	1831 – 1881	Mar. 4, 1881 – Sept. 19, 1881	Chester A. Arthur
21.	Chester A. Arthur *(R)*	1829 – 1886	Sept. 19, 1881 – Mar. 4, 1885	–
22.	Grover Cleveland *(D)*	1837 – 1908	Mar. 4, 1885 – Mar. 4, 1889	Thomas A. Hendricks
23.	Benjamin Harrison *(R)*	1833 – 1901	Mar. 4, 1889 – Mar. 4, 1893	Levi P. Morton
24.	Grover Cleveland *(D)*	1837 – 1908	Mar. 4, 1893 – Mar. 4, 1897	Adlai E. Stevenson
25.	William McKinley *(R)*	1843 – 1901	Mar. 4, 1897 – Sept. 14, 1901	Garret A. Hobart Theodore Roosevelt
26.	Theodore Roosevelt *(R)*	1858 – 1919	Sept. 14, 1901 – Mar. 4, 1909	Charles W. Fairbanks
27.	William H. Taft *(R)*	1857 – 1930	Mar. 4, 1909 – Mar. 4, 1913	James S. Sherman
28.	Woodrow Wilson *(D)*	1856 – 1924	Mar. 4, 1913 – Mar. 4, 1921	Thomas R. Marshall
29.	Warren G. Harding *(R)*	1865 – 1923	Mar. 4, 1921 – Aug. 2, 1923	Calvin Coolidge
30.	Calvin Coolidge *(R)*	1872 – 1933	Aug. 3, 1923 – Mar. 4, 1929	Charles G. Dawes
31.	Herbert Hoover *(R)*	1874 – 1964	Mar. 4, 1929 – Mar. 4, 1933	Charles Curtis
32.	Franklin D. Roosevelt *(D)*	1882 – 1945	Mar. 4, 1933 – Apr. 12, 1945	John N. Garner Henry A. Wallace Harry S. Truman
33.	Harry S. Truman *(D)*	1884 – 1972	Apr. 12, 1945 – Jan. 20, 1953	Alben W. Barkley
34.	Dwight D. Eisenhower *(R)*	1890 – 1969	Jan. 20, 1953 – Jan. 20, 1961	Richard M. Nixon
35.	John F. Kennedy *(D)*	1917 – 1963	Jan. 20, 1961 – Nov. 22, 1963	Lyndon B. Johnson
36.	Lyndon B. Johnson *(D)*	1908 – 1973	Nov. 22, 1963 – Jan. 20, 1969	Hubert H. Humphrey
37.	Richard M. Nixon *(R)*	1913 – 1994	Jan. 20, 1969 – Aug. 9, 1974	Spiro T. Agnew Gerald R. Ford
38.	Gerald R. Ford *(R)*	1913 –	Aug. 9, 1974 – Jan. 20, 1977	Nelson A. Rockefeller
39.	Jimmy Carter *(D)*	1924 –	Jan. 20, 1977 – Jan. 20, 1981	Walter F. Mondale
40.	Ronald Reagan *(R)*	1911 –	Jan. 20, 1981 – Jan. 20, 1989	George Bush
41.	George Bush *(R)*	1924 –	Jan. 20, 1989 – Jan. 20, 1993	Dan Quayle
42.	Bill Clinton *(D)*	1946 –	Jan. 20, 1993 –	Al Gore

*Federalist (*F*), Whig (*W*), Democratic-Republican (*D–R*), Republican (*R*), Democrat (*D*)

George Washington refused a third term as the first U.S. President.

Abraham Lincoln was the first president assassinated in office.

Franklin D. Roosevelt led the U.S. during the Depression and WWII.

John F. Kennedy symbolized the young spirit of the 1960s.

Aztec Empire in Mexico
1400

Inca Empire flourishes in Andes
Late 1400s

Columbus "discovers" Western Hemisphere
1492

John Cabot explores NE coast of North America
1497

Spanish conquer Aztecs
1521

Francisco Coronado explores American SW
1540–42

St. Augustine (Florida) founded by Spaniards
1565

- c. A.D. 30 — Jesus Christ crucified
- 117 — Height of Roman Empire

- c. 320 — Hindu Gupta Dynasty flourishes in India
- 500s — Byzantine Empire at peak
- 622 — Muhammad's flight: Islam established
- c. 800 — Kingdom of Ghana in Africa at peak
- 868 — China makes first printed book

The Statue of Liberty welcomes all who enter New York Harbor.

Sir John A. MacDonald led the first government of Canada as a Dominion.

POPULATION OF LARGEST AMERICAN CITIES (1996 estimate)

RANK	CITY	POPULATION	RANK	CITY	POPULATION	RANK	CITY	POPULATION
1.	New York City, NY	7,380,906	26.	Denver, CO	497,840	51.	Mesa, AZ	344,764
2.	Los Angeles, CA	3,553,638	27.	Portland, OR	480,824	52.	Wichita, KS	320,395
3.	Chicago, IL	2,721,547	28.	Fort Worth, TX	479,716	53.	Toledo, OH	317,606
4.	Houston, TX	1,744,058	29.	New Orleans, LA	476,625	54.	Buffalo, NY	310,548
5.	Philadelphia, PA	1,478,002	30.	Oklahoma City, OK	469,852	55.	Santa Ana, CA	302,419
6.	San Diego, CA	1,171,121	31.	Tucson, AZ	449,002	56.	Arlington, TX	294,816
7.	Phoenix, AZ	1,159,014	32.	Charlotte, NC	441,297	57.	Anaheim, CA	288,945
8.	San Antonio, TX	1,067,816	33.	Kansas City, MO	441,259	58.	Tampa, FL	285,206
9.	Dallas, TX	1,053,292	34.	Virginia Beach, VA	430,385	59.	Corpus Christi, TX	280,260
10.	Detroit, MI	1,000,272	35.	Honolulu, HI	423,475	60.	Newark, NJ	268,510
11.	San Jose, CA	838,744	36.	Long Beach, CA	421,904	61.	Louisville, KY	260,689
12.	Indianapolis, IN	746,737	37.	Albuquerque, NM	419,681	62.	St. Paul, MN	259,606
13.	San Francisco, CA	735,315	38.	Atlanta, GA	401,907	63.	Birmingham, AL	258,543
14.	Jacksonville, FL	679,792	39.	Fresno, CA	396,011	64.	Riverside, CA	255,069
15.	Baltimore, MD	675,401	40.	Tulsa, OK	378,491	65.	Aurora, CO	252,341
16.	Columbus, OH	657,053	41.	Las Vegas, NV	376,906	66.	Anchorage, AK	250,505
17.	El Paso, TX	599,865	42.	Sacramento, CA	376,243	67.	Raleigh, NC	243,835
18.	Memphis, TN	596,725	43.	Oakland, CA	367,230	68.	Lexington-Fayette, KY	239,942
19.	Milwaukee, WI	590,503	44.	Miami, FL	365,127	69.	St. Petersburg, FL	235,988
20.	Boston, MA	558,394	45.	Omaha, NE	364,253	70.	Norfolk, VA	233,430
21.	Washington, DC	543,213	46.	Minneapolis, MN	358,785	71.	Stockton, CA	232,660
22.	Austin, TX	541,278	47.	St. Louis, MO	351,565	72.	Jersey City, NJ	229,039
23.	Seattle, WA	524,704	48.	Pittsburgh, PA	350,363	73.	Rochester, NY	221,594
24.	Nashville-Davidson, TN	511,263	49.	Cincinnati, OH	345,818	74.	Akron, OH	216,882
25.	Cleveland, OH	498,246	50.	Colorado Springs, CO	345,127	75.	Baton Rouge, LA	215,882

THE PROVINCES AND TERRITORIES OF CANADA

PROVINCES	CAPITAL	POPULATION (1996 CENSUS)	(RANK)	AREA IN SQ. MI.	(RANK)	DATE BECAME PROVINCE
Alberta	Edmonton	2,696,826	(4)	255,287	(4)	1905
British Columbia	Victoria	3,724,500	(3)	365,900	(3)	1871
Manitoba	Winnipeg	1,113,898	(5)	250,947	(6)	1870
New Brunswick	Fredericton	738,133	(8)	28,355	(8)	1867
Newfoundland	St. John's	551,792	(9)	156,649	(7)	1949
Nova Scotia	Halifax	909,282	(7)	21,425	(9)	1867
Ontario	Toronto	10,753,573	(1)	412,581	(2)	1867
Prince Edward Island	Charlottetown	134,557	(10)	2,185	(10)	1873
Quebec	Quebec	7,138,795	(2)	594,860	(1)	1867
Saskatchewan	Regina	990,237	(6)	251,866	(5)	1905

TERRITORIES	CAPITAL	POPULATION (1996 CENSUS)	AREA IN SQ. MI.
Northwest Territories	Yellowknife	64,402	1,322,910
Yukon Territory	Whitehorse	30,766	186,661

PRIME MINISTERS OF CANADA

NAME	SERVED	POLITCAL PARTY
Sir John A. Macdonald	1867–1873	Conservative
Alexander Mackenzie	1873–1878	Liberal
Sir John A. Macdonald	1878–1891	Convervative
Sir John Abbott	1891–1892	Conservative
Sir John Thompson	1892–1894	Conservative
Sir Mackenzie Bowell	1894–1896	Conservative
Sir Charles Tupper	1896	Conservative
Sir Wilfrid Laurier	1896–1911	Liberal
Sir Robert Borden	1911–1917	Conservative
Sir Robert Borden	1917–1920	Unionist
Arthur Meighen	1920–1921	Unionist
W.L. Mackenzie King	1921–1926	Liberal
Arthur Meighen	1926	Conservative
W.L. Mackenzie King	1926–1930	Liberal
Richard Bennett	1930–1935	Conservative
W.L. Mackenzie King	1935–1948	Liberal
Louis St. Laurent	1948–1957	Liberal
John Diefenbaker	1957–1963	Progressive Conservative
Lester B. Pearson	1963–1968	Liberal
Pierre E. Trudeau	1968–1979	Liberal
Charles Joseph Clark	1979–1980	Progressive Conservative
Pierre E. Trudeau	1980–1984	Liberal
John Turner	1984	Liberal
Brian Mulroney	1984–1993	Progressive Conservative
Kim Campbell	1993	Progressive Conservative
Jean Chrétien	1993–	Liberal

- 1607 — First British settlement: Jamestown, VA
- 1620 — Pilgrims found colony at Plymouth, MA
- 1626 — Dutch establish city of New Amsterdam
- 1634 — Colony of Maryland founded
- 1636 — Roger Williams founds Providence, RI
- 1664 — English seize New Amsterdam, rename it New York

INTERNATIONAL ORGANIZATIONS

United Nations (UN)
was founded in 1945. Its goals are to maintain international peace and security, and solve cultural, social, and humanitarian problems. There were 51 original members of the UN; in 1997 there were 185 members. Headquarters: New York City. The UN's main organs include: the General Assembly, with representatives of all members; the Security Council, with 15 members, 5 of whom (China, France, Russia, U.K., and U.S.) have permanent seats and 10 of whom are elected for 2 years; and the International Court of Justice, or World Court, which sits in The Hague, Netherlands.

Following are eight of the UN's specialized and related agencies:

Food and Agriculture Organization (FAO)
helps improve production and distribution of food and world dietary standards. Headquarters: Rome, Italy.

International Bank for Reconstruction and Development (IBRD),
or World Bank, provides loans and technical help for economic projects in developing countries. Headquarters: Washington, D.C.

International Monetary Fund (IMF)
promotes monetary cooperation and the expansion of world trade. Headquarters: Washington, D.C.

United Nations Children's Fund (UNICEF)
helps children in developing nations. Headquarters: New York City.

United Nations Educational, Scientific, and Cultural Organization (UNESCO)
promotes exchange of information, ideas, and culture. Headquarters: Paris, France.

United Nations High Commissioner for Refugees (UNHCR)
provides assistance to refugees worldwide. It is based in Geneva, Switzerland.

World Health Organization (WHO)
fights disease and helps improve health standards. Headquarters: Geneva, Switzerland.

World Trade Organization (WTO)
administers trade agreements and attempts to settle disputes. Headquarters: Geneva, Switzerland.

Other international organizations include:

Caribbean Community and Common Market (CARICOM)
was founded in 1973. Members are Antigua and Barbuda, Bahamas, Barbados, Belize, Dominica, Grenada, Guyana, Jamaica, Montserrat, St. Kitts and Nevis, St. Lucia, St. Vincent and the Grenadines, Suriname, and Trinidad and Tobago. Headquarters: Georgetown, Guyana.

The Commonwealth,
founded in 1949, is a loose association of Great Britain and more than 50 other nations that were once part of the British Empire. Mozambique, the most recent member, had not been part of the British Empire. Headquarters: London, England.

Commonwealth of Independent States (CIS),
founded in 1991, is made up of 12 of the 15 former Soviet republics. Members are Armenia, Azerbaijan, Belarus, Georgia, Kazakhstan, Kyrgyzstan, Moldova, Russia, Tajikistan, Turkmenistan, Ukraine, and Uzbekistan. Headquarters: Minsk, Belarus.

European Union (EU),
founded in 1952 with 6 members, was originally a free-trade and customs union. It is now a closer political and economic union. Members are Austria, Belgium, Denmark, Finland, France, Germany, Greece, Ireland, Italy, Luxembourg, the Netherlands, Portugal, Spain, Sweden, and the U.K.

Group of Eight (G-8),
is a group of eight leading industrialized nations that meet to discuss economic issues. Until Russia was admitted in 1997, it was known as the Group of Seven (G-7). The original members are Canada, France, Germany, Japan, Italy, the U.K., and the U.S.

International Criminal Police Organization (Interpol),
founded in 1956, promotes cooperation between police authorities in 177 countries. Headquarters: Lyon, France.

League of Arab States,
also known as the Arab League; promotes economic, social, political, and military cooperation among members. Founded in 1945, it has 22 members, including Palestine, which it considers an independent nation. Headquarters: Cairo, Egypt.

North Atlantic Treaty Organization (NATO)
is a military alliance of Western nations. It was founded in 1949 to defend Western Europe, the U.S., and Canada from military aggression. Members are Belgium, Canada, Denmark, France, Germany, Greece, Iceland, Italy, Luxembourg, the Netherlands, Norway, Portugal, Spain, Turkey, the U.K., and the U.S. Beginning in 1997, plans were made to admit some former Eastern European communist nations into NATO. Headquarters: Brussels, Belgium.

Organization for Economic Cooperation and Development (OECD)
was founded in 1961. Its goals are to promote economic growth, financial stability, and social welfare in its 29 member nations and to assist developing nations. Headquarters: Paris, France.

Organization of African Unity (OAU)
was founded in 1963 to promote unity and cooperation among African nations. It has 53 members. Headquarters: Addis Ababa, Ethiopia.

Organization of American States (OAS)
was founded in 1948. Its major goal is the peaceful settlement of disputes between nations. It has 35 members. Cuba has been suspended from OAS activities since 1962, but not from membership. Headquarters: Washington, D.C.

Organization of Petroleum Exporting Countries (OPEC)
was founded in 1960 to coordinate oil production and prices. Members are Algeria, Indonesia, Iran, Iraq, Kuwait, Libya, Nigeria, Qatar, Saudi Arabia, United Arab Emirates, and Venezuela. Headquarters: Vienna, Austria.

Logo for the League of Arab States, which mediates disputes among its member nations.

Logo for the European Union. This was known as the European Community (EC) until 1994.

The Commonwealth of Independent States is not in itself a state but an alliance of fully independent states.

Since the end of the Cold War in the 1990s, NATO has had to reassess its military role.

1618–48 Thirty Years' War

1644 Start of Manchu rule in China

1700s–1800s Industrial Revolution

1756–63 Seven Years' War

1775–83 Revolutionary War

1789–99 French Revolution

1804–15 Napoleonic Wars

1811–25 Latin American nations win independence

BIOGRAPHIES

Leonardo was not only an artist, but also an inventor, mathematician, engineer, and anatomist.

Picasso was the most famous artist of the 20th century. His work changed the course of modern art.

Chaucer's *Canterbury Tales* is a collection of stories told by pilgrims on their journey to Canterbury.

Brought up in poverty himself, Dickens wrote knowledgeably about the lives of the poor.

ARTISTS

Audubon, John James (1785–1851), a U.S. artist and naturalist, was noted for his paintings of birds.

Botticelli, Sandro (c.1445–1510) was an Italian painter. Works such as *Primavera* (Spring) and the *Birth of Venus* reflect the humanist and classical interests of his time.

Copley, John Singleton (1738–1815) is considered the greatest painter of colonial America. He painted portraits of people such as Paul Revere in natural poses.

Cézanne, Paul (1839–1906), a French painter, started out as an impressionist. His paintings showed the effects of light on objects rather than the objects themselves. He later painted colorful, more solid forms.

Degas, Edgar (1834–1917), a French painter and sculptor, was influenced by impressionism and Japanese woodcuts. He was interested in the human form, and many of his subjects were ballet dancers. His paintings include *The Rehearsal* and *Dance Class.*

Giotto (c.1266–1337), an Italian painter, revived the art of painting in the early Renaissance period. He was especially known for his religious frescoes, including *Life of Christ* and the *Last Judgment.*

Goya y Lucientes, Francisco José de (1746–1828), a Spaniard, painted realistic portraits and scenes from everyday life, including *The Disasters of War.*

Hopper, Edward (1882–1967) painted ordinary American scenes. The people in many of his paintings are often shown as lonely or sad.

Homer, Winslow (1836–1910) is considered one of the greatest U.S. artists. His paintings, including *Breezing Up* and *Gulf Stream*, captured the power and beauty of the sea.

Leonardo da Vinci (1452–1519), an Italian painter and scientist, was a genius. His greatest works include the *Last Supper* and the *Mona Lisa.*

Michelangelo (1475–1564), an Italian painter, sculptor, and architect, created the frescoes on the ceiling of the Sistine Chapel and sculptures of the *Pietà* and *David.*

Monet, Claude (1840–1926), a French painter, was one of the creators of the impressionist movement. Among his most famous works are *Impression: Sunrise*, the Rouen Cathedral series, and the Water Lily series.

Picasso, Pablo (1881–1973), a Spaniard, is thought by many to be the greatest artist of the 20th century. With Georges Braque, he developed cubism, a style in which forms are broken down into geometric shapes.

Pollock, Jackson (1912–56), an American, one of the most influential artists of the 20th century, was an abstract expressionist who made the colors and shapes of his paintings reflect his feelings. Among his works are *Autumn Rhythm.*

Rembrandt (Harmenszoon van Rijn) (1606–69) was the greatest of the Dutch old master painters. He did many group portraits and self-portraits. Among his works are *The Night Watch* and *Syndics of the Cloth Guild.*

Rubens, Peter Paul (1577–1640), a Flemish painter, master of the baroque style. He painted portraits, landscapes, and religious and historical subjects.

Turner, Joseph M. W. (1775–1851) was a British landscape painter. He painted in both watercolors and oils. His atmospheric paintings include *The Fighting Téméraire* and *Old Chain Pier at Brighton.*

Van Gogh, Vincent (1853–90), a Dutch painter, was famous for his use of color. His paintings include *Sunflowers* and *Starry Night.*

Warhol, Andy (1926–87) was a U.S. pioneer in "pop art." He painted pop culture objects, such as Campbell's soup cans, and comic-strip characters.

Wren, Sir Christopher (1632–1723) is considered the greatest English architect. His best-known creation was St. Paul's Cathedral in London.

Wright, Frank Lloyd (1869–1959), the greatest U.S. architect of the 20th century, designed such masterpieces as the Falling Water House and the Guggenheim Museum.

WRITERS

Alcott, Louisa May (1832–88), a U.S. author, is best known for the novel *Little Women*, a story about the four March sisters and their family during the Civil War.

Andersen, Hans Christian (1805–75), a Danish writer, was one of the world's greatest storytellers. He is best known for his fairy tales, such as "The Emperor's New Clothes," "The Snow Queen," "The Little Mermaid," and "The Ugly Duckling."

Austen, Jane (1775–1817), an English novelist, wrote about the middle class of English country life in such novels as *Emma*, *Pride and Prejudice*, and *Sense and Sensibility.*

Cervantes, Miguel (1547–1616) was a Spanish novelist and dramatist. His greatest work, *Don Quixote*, details the life of a poor gentleman who wants to be a knight and do knightly deeds.

Chaucer, Geoffrey (c.1345–1400) was an English poet whose most famous work was a group of stories called the *Canterbury Tales.*

Cooper, James Fenimore (1789–1851) wrote novels about the American frontier in the 1700s. His most famous book was *The Last of the Mohicans.*

Dante Alighieri (1265–1321) was Italy's greatest poet. His most famous work was the *Divine Comedy.*

Dickens, Charles (1812–70) was one of England's greatest novelists. Some of his novels, including *Oliver Twist* and *David Copperfield*, drew attention to the plight of the poor and underprivileged.

1803 Louisiana Purchase doubles size of U.S.

1812–15 War of 1812

1848 U.S. defeats Mexico in Mexican War; California Gold Rush begins

1861–65 North and South fight Civil War

1865 President Abraham Lincoln assassinated; 13th Amendment abolishes slavery

1854 Japan opens its doors to trade with the West

1859 Darwin writes *Origin of Species*

1869 Suez Canal opens

1870 France defeated in Franco-Prussian War

1870–1914 European colonization of Africa and Asia

1894–95 China defeated in Sino-Japanese War

Dickinson, Emily (1830–86)
was one of the most important U.S. poets of the 1800s. She wrote 1,775 poems, but only a few were published when she was alive.

Frost, Robert (1874–1963)
was one of the most important U.S. poets of the 20th century. He wrote about the people and the land of New England. Among his books of poetry are *New Hampshire* and *In the Clearing*.

Goethe, Johann Wolfgang von (1749–1832)
was a poet, novelist, and playwright of unequaled importance in German literature. His greatest work was *Faust*.

Hawthorne, Nathaniel (1804–64),
born in Massachusetts, was one of the most important American writers of the 1800s. His greatest novel was *The Scarlet Letter*.

Henry, O. (1862–1910)
was one of America's foremost short-story writers. His real name was William Sydney Porter. He wrote more than 300 stories, many with surprise endings. One of his most popular stories is "The Gift of the Magi."

Keats, John (1795–1821),
an English poet, wrote beautiful odes, including "To a Nightingale," "On a Grecian Urn," and "To Autumn."

Longfellow, Henry Wadsworth (1807–82)
was a modern language professor and popular poet who wrote poems about American history including such long poems as *The Song of Hiawatha*.

Melville, Herman (1819–91)
was one of the great U.S. writers. He used his experiences as a sailor when writing his most popular books, *Moby Dick* and *Typee*.

Poe, Edgar Allan (1809–49),
a U.S. author, has been called the father of modern mystery and horror stories. His short stories include, "The Fall of the House of Usher," and "The Pit and the Pendulum." Poems include "The Raven" and "The Bells."

Sandburg, Carl (1878–1967)
was one of the most beloved U.S poets, as well as a biographer. His biography of Abraham Lincoln won the 1940 Pulitzer Prize for history.

Shakespeare, William (1564–1616),
an English dramatist and poet, is considered by many to be the world's greatest writer. His plays include *A Midsummer Night's Dream*, *Hamlet*, and *Macbeth*.

Stevenson, Robert Louis (1850–94)
was a versatile Scottish author. He wrote *A Child's Garden of Verses*, and such adventure stories as *Treasure Island* and *Kidnapped*.

Stowe, Harriet Beecher (1811–96),
a U.S. author, was famous for her novel *Uncle Tom's Cabin*. It made a powerful case against slavery.

Swift, Jonathan (1667–1745)
was an English writer whose books poked fun at the silly, cruel behavior of people and governments. His most famous book is *Gulliver's Travels*.

Tolstoy, Count Leo (1828–1910)
was a Russian novelist. Two of his greatest books were *War and Peace* and *Anna Karenina*.

Twain, Mark (1835–1910)
was a popular U.S. novelist and journalist. His real name was Samuel Clemens. Among his bestselling books were *The Adventures of Tom Sawyer* and *The Adventures of Huckleberry Finn*.

Wordsworth, William (1770–1850)
was one of England's greatest poets. His poetry explores the lives of ordinary people in contact with nature. Together with his friend Samuel Taylor Coleridge, he wrote the *Lyrical Ballads*, which included his poem "Tintern Abbey."

COMPOSERS AND MUSICIANS

Bach, Johann Sebastian (1685–1750),
a German, was one of the world's greatest composers. He wrote concertos and sacred cantatas. His masterpieces include the six *Brandenburg Concertos*, *St. Matthew Passion*, and *B Minor Mass*.

Beethoven, Ludwig van (1770–1827),
a German, wrote sonatas, symphonies, choral and chamber music, and concertos. Major works include his Ninth Symphony, the Piano Concerto no. 5, and the opera *Fidelio*.

Berlin, Irving (1888–1989)
was one of the greatest U.S. writers of popular music. He wrote nearly 1,000 songs, including "*Alexander's Ragtime Band*," "*This Is the Army*," and "*God Bless America*."

Bizet, Georges (1838–75),
a French composer, is most famous for his opera *Carmen*.

Brahms, Johannes (1833–97),
a German Romantic composer and gifted pianist, wrote piano sonatas, symphonies, and choral works.

Britten, Benjamin (1913–76),
a British composer, wrote such operas as *Billy Budd* and *Death in Venice*. He also wrote large-scale instrumental works, including *The Young Person's Guide to the Orchestra*.

Copland, Aaron (1900–90),
U.S. composer best known for using jazz and American folk tunes in his classical compositions. His works include the music for such ballets as *Billy the Kid*, *Rodeo*, and *Appalachian Spring*.

Ellington, Duke (1899–1974)
was the greatest U.S. jazz composer. He wrote more than 2,000 jazz compositions, plus concert works, religious music, and scores for theater, ballet, and film.

Gershwin, George (1898–1937)
was one of the most important U.S. songwriters of the 20th century. He produced many concert works and Broadway musicals. Gershwin's best-known works include *Porgy and Bess*, an opera, and *Rhapsody in Blue*, an orchestral work.

Handel, Georg Frideric (1685–1759),
a German-born British composer, was famous for the oratorio *Messiah*. His orchestral works include *Water Music* and *Music for the Royal Fireworks*.

Haydn, Franz Joseph (1732–1809),
an Austrian composer, was the most famous composer of his day, and he is known as the "father of the symphony." His output included 104 symphonies, about 50 concertos, and 84 string quartets, among other works.

Ives, Charles (1874–1954)
was one of the most important U.S. composers of the 20th century. His works

Tolstoy introduced a new form of Christianity into Russia, writing religious works as well as novels.

Tom Sawyer's adventures on the Mississippi River were based on Twain's own boyhood experiences.

Beethoven's music is among the greatest in the world and still influences composers today.

Duke Ellington was one of America's best-known jazz band leaders of the 1930s. He wrote over 50 hits.

U.S. buys Alaska from Russia 1867

Spanish-American War; U.S. annexes Hawaii 1898

U.S. fights in World War I 1917–18

19th Amendment gives women the vote 1920

Great Depression 1930s

U.S. fights in World War II 1941–45

1904–5 Russia defeated in Russo-Japanese War

1912 Chinese overthrow Manchu Dynasty; establish republic

1914–18 World War I

1917 Communists seize power in Russia

1929 Wall Street Crash starts worldwide depression

1933 Hitler comes to power in Germany

1936–39 Civil war in Spain

Mozart began writing music at the age of five. Two years later, he was playing in concerts.

Marie and Pierre Curie devoted their lives to research, spending their own money on equipment.

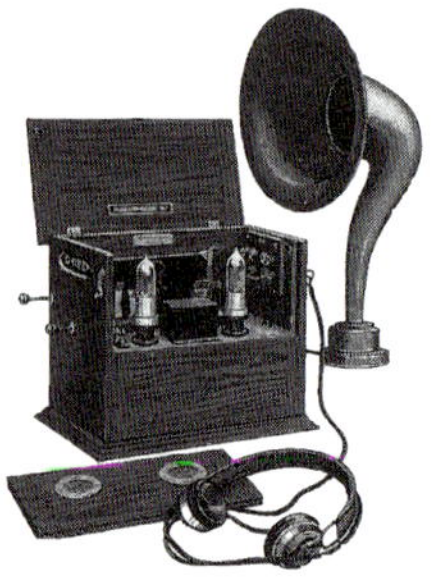

Edison's first phonograph, a recording machine, led to the development of the record player.

Aristotle studied under Plato for 20 years before becoming tutor to Alexander the Great.

included symphonies, sonatas, and orchestral, choral, and chamber music. He also wrote some 150 songs. Many of his compositions used themes from American folk music.

Monteverdi, Claudio (1567–1643),
an Italian composer, wrote *Orfeo*, which is considered to be the first opera.

Mozart, Wolfgang Amadeus (1756–91),
an Austrian, was one of the world's greatest composers. He began composing at the age of five and eventually wrote more than 600 pieces of music, including symphonies, piano concertos, and operas such as *Don Giovanni* and *The Marriage of Figaro*.

Rodgers, Richard (1902–79)
was one of the most successful U.S. composers in the history of entertainment. He wrote the music for such Broadway musicals as *Oklahoma!*, *Pal Joey*, *The King and I*, *South Pacific*, and *The Sound of Music*.

Sousa, John Philip (1854–1932)
wrote so many U.S. marches he was known as the "March King." His most famous works include "The Stars and Stripes Forever," The Washington Post March," and "Semper Fidelis."

Stravinsky, Igor (1882–1971),
a Russian-born U.S. composer, wrote symphonies and operas, as well as the music for such ballets as *The Firebird* and *The Rite of Spring*.

Tchaikovsky, Peter Ilyich (1840–93)
was a Russian composer. He wrote ballet music, symphonies, piano concertos, and operas. Among his best-known works are the ballet *Swan Lake* and his First Piano Concerto.

Verdi, Giuseppe (1813–1901)
was the leading Italian operatic composer of his day. *Rigoletto*, *La Traviata*, and *Aida* are among his best-known works.

Vivaldi, Antonio (c.1675–1741)
was a Venetian violinist and composer. He wrote operas, sacred music, and concertos such as *The Four Seasons*.

Wagner, Richard (1813–83),
a German composer, is best known for his opera cycle *The Ring of the Nibelung*, which consists of four works based on old Germanic mystical legends.

SCIENTISTS AND INVENTORS

Bell, Alexander Graham (1847–1922),
a Scottish-born American, invented the telephone.

Benz, Karl (1844–19129),
a German engineer, built the first practical gasoline-powered automobile.

Copernicus, Nicolaus (1473–1543),
a Polish astronomer, proved that the Earth moves in orbit around the Sun.

Curie, Marie (1867–1934),
a Polish physicist, discovered radium, a radioactive substance. She worked with her husband Pierre.

Daguerre, Louis (1789–1851),
a French painter, invented the first practical photographic process.

Darwin, Charles (1809–82),
a British naturalist, formulated the theory of evolution by natural selection.

Edison, Thomas Alva (1847–1931),
a U.S. inventor, patented more than a thousand inventions, including the telegraph and electric lightbulb.

Einstein, Albert (1879–1955),
a German-born American physicist, changed our view of the universe with his General Theory of Relativity (1915).

Faraday, Michael (1791–1867),
a British physicist and chemist, was a pioneer in the field of electricity. His work made the dynamo and the electric motor possible.

Fermi, Enrico (1901–54),
an Italian nuclear physicist, built the first nuclear reactor.

Fleming, Alexander (1881–1955),
a British bacteriologist, discovered penicillin, the first antibiotic.

Franklin, Benjamin (1706–90),
a U.S. scientist, publisher, and statesman, proved that lightning is a form of electricity.

Galilei, Galileo (1564–1642),
an Italian astronomer and physicist, was the first to use the telescope. He also showed that light objects fall as fast as heavy ones when they are pulled toward the Earth by gravity.

Gutenberg, Johann (c.1400–68),
a German printer, was the first to develop a way to print books with speed and accuracy.

Harvey, William (1578–1657),
a British physician, discovered that the heart acted as a pump to circulate blood through the body.

Kepler, Johannes (1571–1630),
a German astronomer, showed that the planets went around the Sun in elliptical paths.

Marconi, Guglielmo (1874–1937),
an Italian-born British engineer, was the first person to transmit long-distance radio signals.

Mendel, Gregor (1822–84),
an Austrian priest, biologist, and botanist, researched the laws of heredity using pea plants.

Morse, Samuel F.B. (1791–1872),
a U.S. inventor, invented the first successful electric telegraph (1837).

Newton, Isaac (1642–1727),
an English mathematician, devised laws of motion, theorized about gravity, and showed the nature of light and color.

Pasteur, Louis (1822–95),
a French scientist, proved that disease is spread by bacteria, or germs.

Rutherford, Sir Ernest (1871–1937),
a New Zealand-born British physicist, was a pioneer in the study of the atom's structure. His work led to the development of nuclear energy.

Watt, James (1736–1819),
British engineer who improved the steam engine to make it a suitable power plant for all kinds of machinery.

Wright, Orville (1871–1948) and Wilbur (1867–1912),
two U.S. aeronautical engineers, built and flew (1903) the first successful heavier-than-air aircraft.

PHILOSOPHERS AND REFORMERS

Aristotle (384–322 B.C.),
a Greek philosopher, studied under Plato. He opened a school of philosophy in Athens. His work gave rise to the science of logical reasoning.

1950–53 Korean War

1954 School segregation ruled unconstitutional

1962 Cuban missile crisis

1963 President John F. Kennedy assassinated

1965 U.S. combat troops enter Vietnam War

1968 Martin Luther King, Jr. assassinated

1969 Neil Armstrong first to walk on the Moon

1939-45; 1945
World War II; United Nations founded

1949
Communists take over China

1952
EU founded

1957-75
Vietnam War

1979
Islamic Revolution in Iran

1989-90
Democracy sweeps Eastern Europe

1992
Yugoslavia breaks up

1994
Black rule comes to South Africa

Calvin, John (1509-64)
was a French religious reformer and leader of the Protestant Reformation. He believed that all people, not just bishops and kings, should share in religious and political policy making.

Confucius (c. 551-c. 480 B.C.)
was a Chinese philosopher whose teachings on moral responsibility have been a strong influence on Chinese thinking for over 2,000 years.

Gandhi, Mohandas Karamchand (1869-1948),
Indian spiritual and political leader, helped free India from British control through nonviolent resistance. He was known as Mahatma, or "Great Soul."

Gautama, Siddhartha (Buddha) (c. 563-483 B.C.),
Indian religious teacher, founder of Buddhism, one of the world's great religions. He gave up his life as a prince to become a wandering monk in search of enlightenment.

Jesus Christ (c. 4 B.C.-c. A.D. 33)
was the great religious leader on whose teachings the Christian religion was founded.

Joan of Arc, Saint (c. 1412-1431),
French national leader and heroine, believed God had chosen her to free France from English rule and led French armies to many victories.

King, Martin Luther (1929-68)
was a black American minister and leader of the U.S. civil rights movement. King won the 1964 Nobel Peace Prize, but was assassinated four years later.

Luther, Martin (1483-1546)
was a German religious reformer and leader of the Reformation— the religious movement that led to the birth of Protestantism.

Marx, Karl (1818-83)
was a German political philosopher and main founder of the socialist and communist movements. Wrote *The Communist Manifesto*, with Friedrich Engels, and *Das Kapital*.

Montessori, Maria (1870-1952),
Italian educator and doctor, she designed an educational system to help children develop their intelligence and independence. This system is used throughout the world.

Mother Teresa of Calcutta (1910-1997)
was a Roman Catholic nun born in Yugoslavia. She founded a religious order in Calcutta in 1950 called Missionaries of Charity, which has branches in about 30 other countries.

Muhammad (A.D. 570-632)
was an Arabian prophet and founder of the Islamic religion. He felt himself called as God's prophet and preached that there is only one God (Allah).

Nightingale, Florence (1820-1910),
English nursing pioneer, reformed the nursing profession.

Pankhurst, Emmeline (1858-1928)
was an English political reformer. She led the fight for women's right to vote in England.

Plato (c. 427-c.347BC),
a Greek philosopher, founded what is probably the first-ever university, known as the Academy. He wrote *The Republic*, in which he outlined the ideal state or society.

Sanger, Margaret (1883-1966)
was the American leader of the birth control movement.

Socrates (c. 469-399 B.C.),
a Greek philosopher and teacher, devoted himself to seeking truth and goodness.

Stanton, Elizabeth Cady (1815-1902)
was a leader of the U.S. women's rights movement. She also worked for the abolition of slavery.

Wesley, John (1703-91),
English clergyman, founder of Methodism. He traveled over 5,000 miles a year, preaching.

Wilberforce, William (1759-1833)
was an English politician and reformer. He led the fight to abolish slavery in the British Empire.

Wollstonecraft, Mary (1759-97)
was an English author who argued that women should have equal rights to men in her book, *A Vindication of the Rights of Women*.

EXPLORERS

Amundsen, Roald (1872-1928),
a Norwegian, discovered the Northwest Passage and was the first man to reach the South Pole (1911).

Balboa, Vasco Núñez de (1475-1519),
a Spaniard, was the first European to sight the east coast of the Pacific Ocean (1513).

Bird, Richard E. (1888-1957),
a U.S. polar explorer, was the first to fly over the North Pole (1926) and the South Pole (1929).

Cabot, John (c.1461-98),
an Italian-born English explorer, claimed North American territory for England.

Champlain, Samuel de (1567-1635),
a French explorer, explored the Atlantic coast of Canada and founded Quebec (1608).

Columbus, Christopher (1451-1506),
an Italian explorer, discovered the New World while seeking a route to Asia.

Cook, James (1728-79),
an English sea captain, was the first to sight Antarctica and explore the Pacific Ocean.

Cortés, Hernán (1485-1547),
a Spanish explorer, conquered the Aztec Empire of Mexico (1521).

Da Gama, Vasco (c.1469-1524),
Portuguese navigator and explorer, sailed around Africa to India and back to Europe.

Ericsson, Leif (fl. 900-1000),
a Viking sailor, was the first European to land in North America (c.1000).

Livingstone, David (1813-73),
a Scottish explorer, traveled through much of Africa's interior.

Magellan, Ferdinand (c.1480-1521),
a Portuguese explorer, led the first expedition to sail around the world (1519-22). He was killed by natives in the Philippines before the journey was completed.

Peary, Robert E. (1856-1920),
a U.S. explorer, claimed to be the first person to reach the North Pole (1909).

Pizarro, Francisco (c.1475-1541),
a Spanish explorer, conquered the Inca Empire of Peru (1533).

Polo, Marco (c.1254-1324),
a Venetian (Italian) explorer, traveled through Asia and met Kublai Khan, the Mongol emperor.

Elizabeth Cady Stanton began the U.S. women's suffrage movement in 1848.

Gandhi is often called the "father of modern India" for his work in freeing India from British rule.

Vasco da Gama reached India in 1498 by sailing around the Cape of Good Hope in southern Africa.

Henry Morton Stanley, a reporter, found Livingstone (feared dead in Africa) at Lake Tanganyika in 1871.

Vietnam War ends
1975

U.S. invades Panama
1989

U.S. and Allies defeat Iraq in Persian Gulf War
1991

Truck bomb kills 168 in Oklahoma City
1995

U.S. peacekeeping troops arrive in Bosnia
1995

Timothy McVeigh sentenced to death for Oklahoma City bombing
1997

HIGHLIGHTS OF THE 20TH CENTURY

In Germany, Adolf Hitler's aggressive policies led to the outbreak of WW II.

DNA determines which traits children inherit from their parents.

Personal computers became commonly available in the early 1980s.

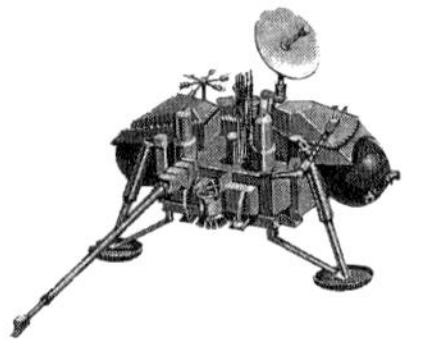

U.S. spacecraft *Viking I* and *2* landed probes on Mars by parachute.

Half of the world's robots, such as this automated arm, are used in Japan.

In 1953, Hillary and Tenzing were the first to scale Mt. Everest.

SPACE EXPLORATION

1957: The Soviet Union launches *Sputnik 1*, the first artificial satellite to orbit the Earth.
1961: Soviet cosmonaut Yuri Gagarin, aboard the *Vostok 1* spacecraft, becomes the first man to orbit the Earth.
1962: Astronaut John H. Glenn, Jr., aboard the *Mercury 6* spacecraft, becomes the first American to orbit the Earth.
1963: Soviet cosmonaut Valentina Tereshkova orbits the Earth in the *Vostok 6* spacecraft, becoming the first woman in space.
1965: Soviet cosmonaut Aleksei Leonov takes the first space walk.
1968: *Apollo 8* becomes the first spacecraft to orbit the Moon.
1969: *Apollo 11* astronauts Neil Armstrong and Edwin Aldrin become the first men to land on the Moon.
1970: *Venera 7*, a Soviet spacecraft, lands on Venus and transmits data back to Earth.
1975: The Soviet Union's *Venera 7* takes the first photographs of the surface of Venus.
1976: *Viking 1* and *Viking 2*, U.S. spacecraft, land on Mars and send photos and data back to Earth.
1977: The United States launches *Voyager 2*, which will later photograph Jupiter (1979), Saturn (1981), Uranus (1986), and Neptune (1989).
1981: The United States launches the space shuttle *Columbia*, the first reusable manned spacecraft.
1986: The U.S. space shuttle *Challenger* blows up shortly after launch, killing all seven astronauts.
1990: The U.S. space probe *Magellan* orbits Venus and sends radar images of the planet back to Earth. The Hubble Space Telescope is launched.
1997: The U.S. Mars *Pathfinder* spacecraft lands on Mars and deploys *Sojourner*, a roving vehicle to analyze Martian rocks and soil.
1998: Water is discovered frozen in rocks on the Moon.

POLITICAL EVENTS

1914: World War I starts when Archduke Francis Ferdinand of Austria is assassinated. The war ends in 1918.
1917: The Communists seize power in Russia during the Russian Revolution.
1929: The Wall Street Crash sets off the Great Depression.
1933: Adolf Hitler becomes the dictator of Germany.
1939: The German invasion of Poland starts World War II.
1941: The United States enters World War II after Japan attacks Pearl Harbor.
1945: World War II ends after the United States drops two atomic bombs on Japan. Tens of millions of people were killed during the war, including six million Jews killed in the Holocaust. The United Nations is founded.
1948: The state of Israel is founded.
1949: The Communists take control of China.
1950: Communist North Korea invades South Korea, starting the Korean War. The fighting ended three years later.
1952: European Community (now European Union), is founded.
1965: U.S. combat troops enter the Vietnam War. The war ends with the defeat of the U.S. in 1973.
1989: Communism begins to collapse in Eastern Europe, with democratic governments replacing communist dictatorships.
1990: Apartheid ends and black rule begins in South Africa.
1991: The Soviet Union ceases to exist and breaks up into 15 independent states.

SCIENCE AND MEDICINE

1905: German-born U.S. physicist Albert Einstein publishes his special theory of relativity.
1913: Hungarian-born pediatrician Bela Schick discovers an immunity test for diphtheria.
1915: Physicist Albert Einstein publishes his general theory of relativity.
1921: Canadian physicians Frederick Banting and Charles Best discover the hormone insulin, a treatment for diabetes.
1928: Scottish bacteriologist Alexander Fleming discovers penicillin, the first antibiotic.
1942: U.S. physicist Enrico Fermi directs the first controlled nuclear reaction.
1945: The first atomic bomb is detonated in New Mexico.
1953: Biologists Francis Crick (U.K.) and James Watson (U.S.) discover the structure of deoxyribonucleic acid (DNA), the actual material that chromosomes are made of.
1954: Harvard University physicians perform the first successful organ (kidney) transplant.
1955: U.S. microbiologist Jonas Salk develops the first vaccine against polio, a crippling disease.
1967: South African surgeon Christiaan Barnard performs the first heart transplant.
1982: U.S. surgeons working at the Utah Medical Center implant the first artificial heart.
1997: Scottish scientists are the first to clone a sheep.

TELECOMMUNICATIONS

1901: Italian-born inventor Guglielmo Marconi, using Morse code-like dot-and-dash signals, sends the first radio message across the Atlantic Ocean.
1915: First transcontinental telephone call between inventor Alexander Graham Bell in New York and his assistant Thomas Watson in San Francisco, over 3,000 miles away.
1906: U.S. engineer Reginald A. Fessendon broadcasts the first radio program of voice and music.
1929: Russian-born American electronic engineer Vladimir Zworykin demonstrates the first electronic television system.
1936: The British Broadcasting Corporation makes the first television broadcasts.
1946: U.S. engineers J. Presper Eckert, Jr. and John W. Mauchly build ENIAC, the first electronic digital computer.
1947: Bell Telephone Laboratories develops the first transistor.
1951: Eckert and Mauchly build UNIVAC I, the first commercially available computer.
1953: Color television broadcast begins in the United States.
Early 1960s: The integrated circuit is developed.
1961: Bell Telephone Laboratories builds the first practical laser.
1965: Early Bird, the first commercial communications satellite, is launched.
1977: The Apple Computer Company introduces the first personal computer.
1983: Cellular phone service begins.

INDEX

Bold numbers before colons refer to volume numbers. Page numbers in bold type refer to key topics. Page numbers in italic type refer to illustrations and maps.

C

D

E

ACKNOWLEDGMENTS

The publishers wish to thank the following for supplying photographs for this book:

ABBREVIATIONS

(*t* = top; *b* = bottom; *c* = center; *l* = left; *r* = right)

PICTURE LIBRARY ABBREVIATIONS

AAA: The Ancient Art & Architecture Collection; **AKG:** AKG UK Ltd; **BAL:** The Bridgeman Art Library; **B&C Alexander:** Bryan & Cherry Alexander; **BC:** Bruce Coleman Collection; **EB/JD:** Eye Ubiquitous/James Davis Travel Agency; **ET:** E.T. Archive; **FLPA:** Frank Lane Picture Agency; **FS:** Frank Spooner Pictures; **GI:** Getty Images; **HL:** The Hutchison Library; **NHPA:** Natural History Photographic Agency; **OSF:** Oxford Scientific Films; **Panos:** Panos Pictures; **PE:** Planet Earth Pictures; **Popper:** Popperfoto; **RGA:** The Ronald Grant Archive; **RHPL:** Robert Harding Picture Library; **SP:** Still Pictures; **SPL:** Science Photo Library

Pages: **viii:** Colorific **1: 1** NHPA, GI *(tr)* **1: 2** RHPL *(tr)*, NHPA *(b)* **1: 3** Still Pictures *(b)* **1: 4** SP *(tl)*, RHPL *(bl)*, Panos *(br)* **1: 4/5** RHPL *(tc)* **1: 5** The British Museum *(b)*, AllSport UK *(tr)* **1: 8** Telegraph Colour Library *(tr)* **1: 9** OSF *(tr)* **1: 10** PE *(tr)* **1: 12** NHPA *(tl)*, PE *(tr)* **1: 16** Popper *(tl)*, BC *(cr)*, NHPA *(bl)* **1: 17** The British Museum *(bl)*, AAA *(br)* **1: 19** RHPL *(b)* **1: 20** NHPA *(cr)*, B&C Alexander *(bc)* **1: 21** RHPL *(cl)*, GI *(cr)*, HL *(br)* **1: 22** AKG *(tr, c)*, BAL *(tl, cl, cr, bl, br)* **1: 23** AKG *(tl, cr)*, ET *(tr)*, ©Duane Hanson/Saatchi Collection *(bl)*, BAL *(br)* **1: 24** SP *(tr)*, NHPA *(bl)*, RHPL *(b)* **1: 25** Panos *(b)* **1: 26** HL *(tl/b)*, FS *(tr)* **1: 27** Panos *(tr, bl)*, BAL *(bc)* **1: 28** Portfolio Pictures *(bl)*, SPL *(tr)*, Space Photo Library *(bc)*, NASA *(br)* **1: 32** SPL *(tl, tr)* **1: 34** PE *(tr)*, OSF *(bc)* **1: 35** PE *(bc)*, NHPA *(br)* **1: 36** Colorific *(tl)*, SP *(bc)* **1: 37** RHPL *(tl)*, Colorific *(tr)*, NHPA *(c)* **1: 40** Virgin *(cl)*, Images Colour Library *(tr)* **1: 43** GI *(tr)* **1: 44** SPL *(tr)***1: 47** NHPA *(cr)* **2: 1** SPL *(br)* **2: 2** Corbis *(tl)*, SPL *(tr)* **2: 3** Zefa *(br)* **2: 6** EB/JD *(tr)*, RHPL *(cl)*, GI *(b)* **2: 7** GI *(cl)*, EB/JD *(br)* **2: 9** Graham Harrison *(tr)*, GI *(cl, br)* **2: 10** OSF *(cl)* **2: 11** BC *(ct, cb)* **2: 12** Zefa *(tr)*, RHPL *(cl/b)*, Robert Estall Photo Library *(cr)* **2: 13** BC *(cl)*, RHPL *(br)* **2: 14** Panos *(tr)*, HL *(b)* **2: 15** HL *(cl)*, SuperStock *(br)* **2: 16** AllSport UK *(tr)* **2: 17** Ford Motor Company *(tr)* **2: 18** RGA *(tl, ct, cb)*, Portfolio Pictures *(tr)*, SP *(br)* **2: 22** SPL *(l)* **2: 23** The National Museum of Ireland *(tl)*, AAA *(c)*, BAL *(bl)* **2: 24** RHPL *(tr)*, Panos *(b)* **2: 25** GI *(tr, b)*, Panos *(cl)* **2: 27** BC *(tr)*, SP *(cl)*, Image Bank *(b)* **2: 28** BC *(b)* **2: 29** RHPL *(tc)*, GI *(tr, bl)*, RHPL *(br)* **2: 30** Panos *(tr, bl, br)* **2: 31** GI *(c, bcl)*, Zefa *(bl)*, FS *(bcr)*, Rex Features *(br)* **2: 32** Amnesty International *(tl)*, Popper *(tr)*, Corbis *(b)* **2: 33** Corbis *(tl)*, AFP *(bl)*, Camera Press *(br)* **2: 34** Peter Newark Library *(tl)* **2: 38** RHPL *(tr)*, Camera Press *(cl)* **2: 39** Zefa *(tc)*, FS *(tr)*, GI *(c)*, RHPL *(br)* **2: 40** RHPL *(c)* **2: 41** Corbis *(b)* **2: 42** AKG *(tr)* **2: 43** SPL *(tl, bl)* **2: 44** GI *(tr)* **2: 45** Camera Press *(cl, bl)*, AKG *(br)* **2: 47** Corbis *(tr)* GI *(cr)* **2: 48** SPL *(tl)*, AKG *(tr)* **3: 2** Travel Ink *(tr)* **3: 8** RHPL *(br)* **3: 10** Allsport UK/Vandystadt *(bl)*, Performing Arts Library *(br)* **3: 11** EB/JD *(tl)*, Rex Features *(tr)*, Performing Arts Library *(c, br)* **3: 12** Popper *(b)* **3: 13** GI *(tl)* **3: 14** RHPL *(tl)* **3: 18** FS *(tl)*, SPL *(bl)* **3: 19** Farmers Weekly *(br)* **3: 24** Rex Features *(b)* **3: 25** Panos *(tr)*, GI *(b)* **3: 26** Panos *(b)* **3: 27** Panos *(tl)*, GI *(tr)*, Rex Features *(b)* **3: 28** Panos *(br)* **3: 29** Panos *(tl)*, EB/JD *(cl)*, GI *(cr, b)* **3: 30** GI *(l, b)* **3: 31** Simon Farrell *(tr)* **3: 37** GI *(cr)* **3: 38** RHPL *(tr)* **3: 40** Popper *(tl)*, Colorsport *(tr)*, UPI *(cl)* **3: 42** FLPA *(tr)*, GI *(b)* **3: 43** FLPA *(br)* **3: 44** Zefa *(tl)*, GI *(tr)*, Rex Features *(bl)* **3: 45** GI *(tr)*, RHPL *(cl)*, Rex Features *(b)* **4: 1** W.J. Hatt Ltd, The Institute of Explosive *(tl, tc, bl, bc, br)* **4: 2** Topham *(cl)* **4: 3** Popper *(tl, ct, bl)*, Camera Press *(cb)*, Corbis *(bl)* **4: 6** NHPA *(tr)* **4: 8** FLPA *(cr)* **4: 13** NHPA *(tr)* **4: 14** RHPL *(bl)*, **4: 14/15** GI *(c)* **4: 15** GI *(c)* **4: 16** Telegraph Colour Library *(tr)* **4: 17** Robin Keeley *(tl)*, Topham *(cl)* **4: 18** GI *(tl)* **4: 20** GI *(tr, cl, b)* **4: 21** FS *(tl)*, Popper *(cl)*, RHPL *(cr)* **4: 24** SPL *(tr)* **4: 25** SPL *(tl)* **4: 26** SP *(bl)*, Telegraph Colour Library *(bcl, br)*, GI *(bcr)* **4: 27** Popper *(tr)* **4: 28** Zefa *(tr)*, FS *(cl)*, RHPL *(b)* **4: 29** Popper *(cl)*, GI *(b)* **4: 32** Sonia Halliday Photographs *(cl)* **4: 33** SPL *(tr, bc)*, The Wallace Collection, London *(cl)* **4: 34** RHPL *(cr)*, Topham *(bl)* **4: 35** NHPA *(tl)* **4: 36** Corbis *(cl)*, GI *(b)* **4: 37** Corbis *(tr, cr)* **4: 38** GI *(tr, b)* **4: 39** Popper *(tl)*, RHPL *(cl)*, Panos *(br)* **4: 41** RHPL *(tr)* **4: 42** NHPA *(tr, cl)*, PE *(tl, bcl, bcr)*, GI *(cr)* **4: 45** RHPL *(tr)* **4: 48** FS *(tr)*, GI *(b)* **5: 1** BC *(tr)* **5: 2** Image Bank *(b)* **5: 3** GI *(br)* **5: 4** Transcolour *(tr)* **5: 5** GI *(tr)*, Panos *(bl)*, Zefa *(br)* **5: 6** OSF *(tr)* **5: 7** EB/JD *(t, c, bc)*, Panos *(tc, b)* **5: 8** GI *(tl)*, FS *(cl)* **5: 9** Image Bank *(tc)* **5: 12** Panos *(tr)*, GI *(b)* **5: 13** Panos *(c)* Image Bank *(bl)* **5: 14** Colorific Photo Library *(tl)*, GI *(tr)*, FS *(b)* **5: 15** OSF *(tl)*, Corbis *(tr)*, Panos *(bl)* **5: 16** GI *(cl, bl)*, Panos *(cr)* **5: 18** GI *(tl)* **5: 20** RHPL *(tr)*, Panos *(cr)* **5: 21** OSF *(cr, br)* **5: 22** OSF, BC *(br)* **5: 24** FS *(tr)* **5: 25** BAL *(tr)* **5: 26** GI *(cl, bl)*, The Houghton's Horses *(br)* **5: 27** GI *(tr)* **5: 28** RHPL *(cl)*, GI *(b)* **5: 29** FLPA *(tr)*, GI *(cl)*, Network Photography/Mike Abraham *(bl)* **5: 30** GI *(b)* **5: 31** FS *(cr)*, John Ferro Sims *(bl)* **5: 32** GI *(tr, b)*, Panos *(cl)* **5: 33** RHPA *(cr)*, Zefa *(b)* **5: 34** Zefa *(tr)* **5: 35** GI *(tr, cl)*, Image Bank *(bl)*, Colorific Photo Library *(cb)* **5: 37** Panos *(cl)*, PE *(bl)*, GI *(br)* **5: 38** SPL *(tl)* **5: 40** EB/JD *(tl)*, BAL *(b)* **5: 41** RHPL *(tl)*, Zefa *(tr, bl)*, The Research House *(cl)* **5: 42** Image Bank *(tl)* **5: 45** Zefa *(tr, cr)*, Corbis *(tl)*, Image Bank *(cl)*, OSF *(bl, bc)* **5: 46** Image Bank *(tl)* **6: 4** SPL *(tr)* **6: 5** HL *(cl)*, Panos *(bl)*, RHPL *(br)* **6: 9** Image Bank *(tr)* **6: 10** Panos *(tr)* **6: 11** Alpha *(c)*, A.C. Edwards *(bl)* **6: 12** Glaxo Group Research *(tr)* **6: 13** SPL *(tr, b)* **6: 15** AAA *(cr, br)* **6: 16** Telegraph Colour Library *(tl)* **6: 17** South American Pictures *(tr)*, Spectrum Colour Library *(cl)*, Panos *(bl)* **6: 18** SPL *(l)* **6: 19** SPL *(l)*, Leo Electron Microscope *(tr)*, Leica UK *(bc)* **6: 21** RHPL *(tr)*, Panos *(b)* **6: 22** HL *(c)* **6: 23** Spectrum Colour Library *(tl)*, FS *(tr)*, HL *(bc)* **6: 24** PE *(bl)* **6: 25** OSF *(tr)* **6: 26** SP *(tl)* **6: 31** OSF *(br)* **6: 36** Zefa *(t)*, Redferns *(cl, bl, br)* **6: 37** RHPL *(b)* **6: 38** Edinburgh University *(cr)*, Keith Saunders Photography *(bc)* **6: 43** Corbis *(tr)* **6: 45** FS *(bl)* **6: 47** Spectrum Colour Library *(tc, c)*, FS *(bl)* **6: 48** Panos *(cl, b)* **7: 1** Panos *(tr)*, HL *(bl)* **7: 2** NHPA *(bl)* **7: 3** Panos *(tl)*, HL *(tr)*, Zefa *(bl)* **7: 4** Popper *(tr)* **7: 5** SP *(tr)* **7: 8** SPL *(tr)* **7: 9** AllSport *(cr)* Topham *(b)* **7: 10** Topham *(tl)* **7: 11** AllSport UK *(tr, cr)* **7: 13** SPL *(tl)* **7: 15** HL *(tr)*, Panos *(cl, c)* **7: 16** Polaroid *(cl)*, Ixus *(bl)*, BAL *(b)* **7: 17** Science & Society Picture Library *(tr)*, Nikon UK *(br)* **7: 18** HL *(tr)* **7: 21** The Kobal Collection *(bl)* **7: 24** ICI *(b)* **7: 25** NHPA *(tl, tr)* **7: 26** Corbis (t) **7: 27** HL *(b)* **7: 29** AAA *(cl)* **7: 31** Popper *(cr)* **7: 35** NHPA *(cl)* **7: 36** PE *(tr)* **7: 38** SP *(tl)*, Jean-Loup Charmet *(tr)*, Popper *(bl)* **7: 39** HL *(b)* **7: 40** BAL *(cr, bl)* **7: 42** GI *(cr)* **7: 48** Rex Features *(tl)*, Popper *(tr)*, GI *(cl)* **8: 1** PE *(tr)* **8: 2** NHPA *(bl)*, HL *(br)* **8: 4** GI *(tl)*, HL *(bc)* **8: 5** SPL *(tl, cl)*, The Kobal Collection *(tc)*, Honda Motor Company *(tr)* **8: 6:** NHPA *(tr)* **8: 7** NASA *(tr)* **8: 9** Zefa *(tr)*, GI *(cr)* **8: 10** Novosti London *(tr)*, RHPL *(b)* **8: 11** HL *(br)* **8: 12** Rex Features *(tl)*, Novosti London *(cl)*, HL *(bl, br)* **8: 14** GI *(tr, b)* **8: 15** RHPL *(bl)*, FLPA *(br)* **8: 16** AKG *(tl)*, Rex Features *(tr)*, ©Andy Goldworthy *(cl)*, GI *(b)* **8: 17** GI *(tl, cl)*, HL *(br)* **8: 18** HL *(cr)*, Spectrum Colour Library *(br)* **8: 22** Zefa *(tr)* **8: 25** RHPL *(tr)*, AAA *(c)*, Christie's Images *(cr)* **8: 26** GI *(tr, b)* **8: 29** Travel Ink *(tl)* **8: 30** BAL *(tr)*, Mary Evans Picture Library *(br)* **8: 31** SPL *(tl)*, AKG *(b)* **8: 32** OSF *(tc)* **8: 33** NHPA *(tr)* **8: 34** Zefa *(b)* **8: 35** Topham *(tr)* **8: 39** Popper *(b)* **8: 40** RHPL *(cl, tr)*, GI *(b)* **8: 41** FS *(bl)*, RHPL *(cr)* **8: 42** South American Library *(tr, cl, b)* **8: 43** HL *(tl)*, South American Library *(bl)*, Panos *(br)* **8: 44** Panos *(tl, b)*, South American Library *(tr)* **8: 45** South American Library *(tr, c)*, HL *(b)* **8: 46** Panos *(bl)* **8: 47** Panos *(tl, c)*, HL *(tr)* **9: 1** SPL *(tr)* **9: 2** SPL *(l)* **9: 4** GI *(tr)*, HL *(cl)*, RHPL *(b)* **9: 5** HL *(b)* **9: 7** NHPA *(tl)* **9: 9** Sporting Pictures *(tr)*, AllSport UK *(br)* **9: 10** Sporting Pictures *(tc)* **9: 13** NHPA *(tr)* **9: 14** SPL *(tl)*, GI *(tr)* **9: 16** HL *(cl)*, Panos *(bl)* **9: 18** AKG *(tr)*, RHPL *(b)* **9: 20** RHPL **9: 22** SPL *(b)* **9: 23** Zefa *(tr)* **9: 24** Mary Evans Picture Library *(tl)*, British Telecom *(cl)*, GI *(bl)* **9: 25** Corbis *(tr, br)*, Philips UK *(cl)* **9: 27** Simmons Ltd *(tc)*, SPL *(br)* **9: 29** AKG *(tr)*, SPL *(bl)*, RHPL *(br)* **9: 34** Topham *(tr)* **9: 35** Panos *(cl)*, RGA *(cr)*, RHPL *(b)* **9: 36** GI *(tr)* **9: 37** Panos *(b)* **9: 40** SPL *(cl)* **9: 41** FS *(br)* **9: 43** Telegraph Colour Library *(tr)* **9: 44** Greyhound Ltd *(tr)* **9: 45** GI *(bl)* **9: 46** Popper *(cl)*, RHPL *(tr)*, British Tourist Authority *(b)* **9: 47** British Tourist Authority *(tl)*, HL *(bl)*, RHPL *(br)* **9: 48** FS *(cr)*, Popper *(b)* **10: 1** Panos *(tr)*, RHPL *(bl, br)* **10: 2** RHPL *(tl, cl)*, Zefa *(br)* **10: 3** RHPL *(cl, br)* **10: 4** RHPL *(tl, cl)*, Corbis *(cr)*, Redfern *(b)* **10: 5** SPL *(tl)* **10: 6** Popper *(b)* **10: 7** Sanyo UK *(tl)*, SPL *(tr, cl)*, Sony *(br)* **10: 10** HL *(tl)* **10: 14** Topham *(br)* **10: 15** HL *(tc)* **10: 16** Corbis *(tl)* **10: 17** SPL *(tr)* **10: 19** SPL *(tc)* **10: 21** SPL *(tl)* **10: 25** RHPL *(tr)*, SPL *(b)* **10: 27** NHPA *(tc)* **10: 28** Corbis *(tr)*, Corbis *(b)* **10: 29** GI *(tl)*, Corbis *(tr)*, Popper *(bl)*, Corbis *(cr)* **10: 33** Corbis *(bl)* **10: 34** PE *(br)* **10: 35** SPL *(tr, bl)* **10: 36:** Marwell Zoo *(br)*

Illustrators

Julian Baker Illustration, Julian Baum, Michelle Brand, Andy Burton, Tom Connell, Maggie Downer, Richard Draper, Andrew Farmer, Chris Forsey, Mick Gillah, Trevor Hill, Karen Hiscock, Christian Hook, Kevin Jones Associates, Ruth Lindsay, Ceri Llewellyn, Kevin Maddison, Nicki Palin, Peter Ross, Peter Sarson, Mike Saunders, Ron Tiner, Martin Woodward, *Black Hat*: Kevin Lyles, *Blue Chip*: Keith Harmer, *David Lewis Agency*: Mark Stacey, *J.M. & A*: Steinar Lund, *Linda Rogers Associates*: Peter Dennis, *Linden Artists*: Lindsay Graham, Richard Hook, Sebastian Quigley, Clive Spong, *Specs Art*: Richard Berridge, *Virgil Pomfret*: Luigi Galanti, *W.L.A*: Cy Baker, Derick Bown, Robin Budden, Robin Carter, Barry Croucher, Sandra Doyle, Brin Edwards, David Hardy, Dan Harvey, Philip Hood, Ian Jackson, Bridgette Jones, Rachel Lockwood, Pond/Giles, Jonathan Potter, Steve Roberts, Andrew Robinson, Mike Rowe, Chris Shields, Paul Staveley, Mark Stewart, Mike Taylor, Richard Tibbitts, Chris Turnbull, Simon Turvey, David Woods

The publishers would also like to thank the following for their help in supplying information used as visual reference:

Pages: **1: 6-7** Boeing Aircraft Corporation (Boeing 747); **1: 11** Zoological Society of London (fire salamander cutaway); **1: 17** Geoscan Research (scanner); **1: 19** Ove Arup & Partners (Sydney Opera House); **1: 30-31** W.M. Keck Observatory (Keck observatory); **2: 14-15** John Willoughby, The Mustang Owners Club of Great Britain, Selby (Mustang); **4: 2** Fullwood Ltd (milking shed); **4: 46** Bell Helicopter Textron (helicopter cutaway); **5: 4** Dyson Appliances Ltd (Dyson vacuum cleaner cutaway); **5: 6** The Hovercraft Museum Trust; **6: 2-3** Otis plc, Ove Arup & Partners (elevator); **6: 12-13** Picker International Ltd, Siemens Medical Engineering (CAT scanner); **7: 4** Nuclear Electric (nuclear reactor); **7: 8** British Petroleum (platform); **7: 9-11** Olympic Museum; **8: 25** Balco Ltd (electroplating system); **9: 26** British Telecom (wall telephone); **9: 41** Ford Motor Company (people carrier)